MY FIRST COACH

ALSO BY GARY MYERS

Brady vs Manning
The Catch
Coaching Confidential

MY FIRST COACH

Inspiring Stories of
NFL Quarterbacks and Their Dads

GARY MYERS

GRAND CENTRAL
PUBLISHING

NEW YORK   BOSTON

Grand Central Publishing
Hachette Book Group
1290 Avenue of the Americas, New York, NY 10104
grandcentralpublishing.com
twitter.com/grandcentralpub

First Edition: August 2017

Grand Central Publishing is a division of Hachette Book Group, Inc. The Grand Central Publishing name and logo is a trademark of Hachette Book Group, Inc.

The publisher is not responsible for websites (or their content) that are not owned by the publisher.

The Hachette Speakers Bureau provides a wide range of authors for speaking events. To find out more, go to www.hachettespeakersbureau.com or call (866) 376-6591.

Library of Congress Control Number: 2017938902

ISBNs: 978-1-4555-9846-5 (hardcover); 978-1-4555-9847-2 (ebook)

Printed in the United States of America

LSC-C

10 9 8 7 6 5 4 3 2 1

To Allison, Michelle, Emily, and Andrew

CONTENTS

INTRODUCTION

Tom Brady was by his locker getting dressed for practice a few days before the New England Patriots would beat the Pittsburgh Steelers in the AFC Championship Game in 2017. He had been suffering in silence for more than a year after his mother, Galynn, was diagnosed with cancer. His closest friends on the team and in the front office knew, as well as a few others. I asked him how his mother was doing.

"Better," he said. "Thanks for asking."

His father, Tom Brady Sr., had always been Tom's most reliable and valued support system, but he had been to just one game all season, and that was when the Patriots played the San Francisco 49ers in Santa Clara, just a short ride from the Brady home in San Mateo. His father was incredibly devoted to his mother and didn't make any trips to Foxborough during the 2016 regular season, and he wouldn't be attending the championship game in Foxborough, either.

Tom understood. He knew his father had his priorities in the correct order.

"My dad is a great guy," he said quietly by his locker.

He has always felt that way. They have been each other's best friend. When Brady was deciding which college to attend, it came down to Michigan and Cal-Berkeley. Tom Sr. didn't want to influence his son's decision and then be held responsible if things didn't work out. Privately, he was rooting for Cal, just thirty-five miles from his front door. He figured his son would play football on Saturdays and play golf with him on Sundays.

Tom decided on Michigan. "It literally broke my heart," Tom Sr. said.

Eight weeks of psychological counseling to deal with the separation helped Tom Sr. He and Galynn attended 90 percent of Tom's games at Michigan, home and away, even when he wasn't starting. In his first four years as the Patriots starter, they were at every one of his games. Then it was just home games. Then it was just Tom Sr., as he combined business in the Boston office of his estate planning company with Patriots home games.

Brady Sr. was outspoken in defending his son during the NFL's $5 million investigation of deflated footballs in 2015 that became known as Deflategate. Tom Sr. was likely saying what Tom was thinking but couldn't say himself. Tom Sr. phoned into a San Francisco radio show and called Commissioner Roger Goodell "a flaming liar."

Even if Brady agreed with his father, he would never say it. "Dad," he said, "you're not doing me any favors."

It's one of the few times in Brady's life he could say that to his father.

My First Coach explores the important relationship between quarterbacks and their fathers. It provides many life lessons for boys and girls and mothers and fathers through the experiences of some of the best-known and most interesting quarterbacks of this generation.

What parent can't relate to working their schedule around driving their kids to baseball, football, basketball, and soccer practices and games? Or sitting in the stands trying not to make it too obvious which kid is theirs?

Every parent knows the anxiety of not seeing their son or daughter on the field and thinking the coach is being unfair. It is not limited to kids with minimal athletic ability. Joe Flacco, who would go on to become a first-round draft pick and Super Bowl MVP, couldn't get off the bench at Pitt and had to transfer to Delaware. Joe Montana's older son, Nathaniel, hardly played in high school.

There is more than one way to raise a quarterback. Some fathers want to be involved in every aspect of their sons' athletic lives. Some like to coach. Others take a step back. Even others are overbearing—confronting coaches and complaining about playing time. Indifference is not a trait I found in football fathers. Indifference is not what their sons wanted.

The closeness of the Brady family became evident on the Monday night of Super Bowl LI week in Houston in 2017. Brady was asked who his hero was.

"That's a great question," he said. "I think my dad is my hero, because he's someone I've looked up to every day."

As he was answering, Brady became choked up and teary-eyed.

3

His mother's health issues and his father's dedication to her greatly contributed to his emotions.

"He was just a great example for me, and he was always someone who supported me in everything I did, to come home at night and bring me out, hit me ground balls and fly balls. I loved baseball growing up," Brady said. "And to have a chance to go to the 49ers game on the weekend with him and my mom and throw the ball in the parking lot before the games, those are memories that I'll have forever."

Tom Sr. and Galynn arrived in Houston for the Super Bowl at the end of the week after she received medical clearance to attend her first game of the year. When Brady made those comments about his father, Tom Sr. was back home in San Mateo and was deeply touched.

"I think every father relishes time with their sons, and you never know if the son relishes time with his father," he said. "For me to hear he respects me, and as much as I respect him, is the most satisfying feeling that I could ever have."

Like his son, Brady Sr. is emotional when discussing their relationship.

"I remember when he was still in high school and I would go in to wake him up in the morning so we could go play golf," he said. "It was always the greatest joy for me that he wanted to play golf with me. Years later, he made the comment that 'I never wanted to stay out late out on Friday night because I wanted to play golf with my dad Saturday morning.'"

He thought about that for a second. He wanted to grasp the full meaning. "It's more than gratifying," he said. "It's really a fulfillment of my dream. I love every minute I can spend with my son." He knows he's not the only father so fortunate that his son feels that way, and he never takes it for granted. "Many dads that I know love hanging with their kids," he said.

The end of Deflategate finally arrived when Brady was on the podium next to Patriots owner Robert Kraft accepting the Vince Lombardi Trophy from Goodell after he wiped out the biggest deficit in Super Bowl history—25 points—and beat the Atlanta Falcons in overtime. It was the end of two years of aggravation after Brady Sr. felt his son was falsely accused by Goodell. "There's been a lot of pent-up emotions for two years. It was a cathartic time," he said. "Everything that we could have possibly hoped for and more was realized in that moment seeing him up there on the podium."

Tom Brady Sr. has lived the dream of any parent. He has seen his son on the Super Bowl championship stage five times and in the Super Bowl seven times, giving him one more title and three more appearances than any other starting quarterback in NFL history. Yet, it's unrealistic for all fathers to see their sons achieve greatness. Tom Sr. is a lucky man.

My First Coach takes you on a memorable journey; there are success stories and stories of deep disappointment. There's a stop at Phil Simms's home office in Franklin Lakes, New Jersey. Initially, my plan was to talk to him about his relationship with his two sons, Chris and Matt, both of whom made it to the NFL. I have known Simms since the New York Giants drafted him in 1979 but had never heard him talk about his own family life as a kid growing up in Louisville. His childhood was so compelling that it became a big part of the chapter about him in this book. I didn't know that his father was an alcoholic. I didn't know Phil had a brother and a sister who died way too young as adults.

I went to visit Michigan coach Jim Harbaugh, the son of a lifelong coach. His parents, Jack and Jackie, moved to a house around the corner from Jim and his family in Ann Arbor in 2016, just before his second season back at his alma mater. Jack's outgoing personality is much closer to that of his other son, John, the coach of the Baltimore Ravens, than it is to Jim's. One thing is clear: Dad is thrilled that his boys went into the family business. Do you like hearing the Harbaughs' chant, "Who's Got It Better Than Us?" and then their teams reply, "Nobody"? You can thank Jack for that. One of Jack's ten-year-old buddies he played sandlot baseball with when they were kids came up with that, and it's become the Harbaugh rallying cry.

Joe Montana is proud that his sons, Nate and Nick, played college football, even if they attended seven colleges between them looking for the ideal spot to develop their talent. The boys did not have their father's skill set and were further burdened by the expectations of the family name. They survived difficult times that built character even if neither made it to the NFL. Joe felt guilty for years because he believed he had sent Nate to the wrong high school and not given him the best chance to succeed. He didn't make the same mistake with Nick.

I decided to include Ryan Fitzpatrick in this book. He may not have achieved the same level of success as other quarterbacks featured here, but none of the others have a degree from Harvard. He is the only Harvard quarterback to ever start a game in the NFL. What kind of upbringing did he have that allowed him to excel in academics—20 points short of a perfect SAT score—and then play more than ten years in the NFL?

Fathers can certainly provide inspiration and motivation. Brett Favre was very close to his father, Irv. Brett was in Oakland for a Monday night game against the Raiders in 2003. The day before the game, Irv Favre suffered a heart attack behind the wheel of his car in their hometown of Kiln, Mississippi, and drove into a ditch. Authorities believe the heart attack and not the accident killed him. Favre told teammates hours later that he would remain with the team and play in the game.

"For about five minutes there was some indecision on whether or not I was going to play," Favre said. "It didn't take long for me to say, 'You've got to play in this game.'"

He not only played, he was incredible. In the first half, he completed 15 of 18 passes for 311 yards and four touchdowns. The Packers led 31–7. Favre finished 22 of 30 for 399 yards and four touchdowns in a 41–7 victory. He played because he knew his father, his biggest fan, would have wanted him to play. Favre said it was the best game he ever played in. It was also probably the best game he ever played.

Every pass was exactly where it was supposed to be.

"I love him so much and I love this game," he said after the game. "It meant a great deal to me, my dad, to my family; and I didn't expect this kind of performance. But I know he was watching tonight."

Favre was elected to the Pro Football Hall of Fame in his first year of eligibility in 2016. He gave a speech that said much about his relationship with his father. Brett mentioned that Irv once had told Favre's wife, Deanna, that he wanted to be the one to introduce Brett at the Hall of Fame. Until then, Favre said, he had never thought much about the Hall of Fame, but he was determined to make his father's wish come true.

In his speech, he said, "My father was short on praise and long on tough love. If he was ever to praise me, I was not to hear it. It was always, 'You can do better.' He was always pushing me to be better. And that was okay. Never did I hear him say, 'Son, you've arrived. You're the best. That was awesome. Great game.' It was always, 'Yeah, but...'"

He said he never would have made the Hall of Fame without his father. Irv was also his high school coach. "He taught me toughness," Favre said. "Boy, did he teach me toughness. Trust me, there was no room for crybabies in our house. He taught me teamwork, and by all means no player was ever more important than the team."

After he played poorly in a game, he heard his father tell three of his assistant coaches in the middle of the week, "I can assure you one thing about my son—he will play better. He will redeem himself. I know my son. He has it in him."

Then Favre said in his Hall of Fame speech, "I never let him know that I heard that. I never said that to anyone else. But I thought to myself: 'That's a pretty good compliment, you know?' My chest kind of swelled up. And again, I never told anyone. But I never forgot that statement and that comment that he made to those other coaches. And I want you to know, Dad, I spent the rest of my career trying to redeem myself."

Aaron Rodgers, who succeeded Favre as the Packers starting quarterback in 2008, was close with his family for the early portion of his NFL career. Aaron's parents and his brothers were pictured on the field with Aaron when the Packers were in Super Bowl XLV in Arlington, Texas, in February 2011. But Aaron and his family subsequently became estranged, and there was no communication starting in late 2014.

"Fame can change things," Ed Rodgers, a chiropractor and Aaron's father, told the *New York Times*. Summing up where the relationship was headed, he said, "It's complicated. We're all hoping for the best."

Irv Favre was able to see his son win a Super Bowl. Harrison Wilson III, known as Harry, wasn't so fortunate. His son Russell Wilson, the quarterback of the Seattle Seahawks, defeated Peyton Manning in the Super Bowl following the 2013 season and nearly defeated Brady the next year. Wilson's father died in 2010 at the age of fifty-five following complications from diabetes. Wilson III played wide receiver at Dartmouth, then went to law school in 1977 and was in the San Diego Chargers training camp in 1980 and nearly made the team.

"I always believe he's there with me, no matter what stadium we're playing in, home or away," Russell Wilson said. "I believe my dad has the best seat in the house."

There's likely been no father more overbearing than Marv Marinovich, who provides a treacherous blueprint of fathers who want their sons to succeed so badly it turns out to be detrimental. From the day Todd Marinovich was born on July 4, 1969, his father raised him to be a quarterback. He was dubbed

"Robo QB." There were stories of Marv stretching Todd as an infant to become more limber. He put him through difficult conditioning drills and football workouts when he was probably too young for such a regimen. Marv controlled his son's diet, and he used computer analysis to try to build the perfect football player. Marv once talked about the vitamins and minerals he and his wife were taking even before Todd was conceived.

Marv was a former player at the University of Southern California and lineman for the Oakland Raiders and later was hired by Raiders owner Al Davis as the team's strength and conditioning coach. "To me, the Robo quarterback means the guy has all the equipment," Marv told the *New York Times* in 1990. "Everything in sync. Everything balanced. The perfect machine. From a training standpoint, not that Todd is that, but the appearance of that is a positive situation. You could never be too good with your mechanics of throwing. You can never be too focused, mentally. You can never have too good a vision. You strive for those things. The idea of Robo, the ultimate decision-making trigger machine."

Todd Marinovich went on to be USC's quarterback and was a first-round draft choice of the Raiders in 1991. Favre went in the second round, nine spots after Marinovich. Robo QB? "I don't know what that really means," Todd told the *New York Times*. "I think people can get the false idea of what I'm all about."

He never outwardly resented his father's role in his development. He once said people got the wrong impression of Marv. But he lasted only two years with the Raiders and his NFL career was over. Eight touchdown passes. He later played in the Canadian Football League and the Arena Football League. He's battled drug issues, and in October 2016 he was charged in California with trespassing, public nudity, and drug possession after he was found naked in the backyard of somebody he did not know.

Oakland Raiders quarterback Derek Carr and Tampa Bay Buccaneers quarterback Jameis Winston have a long way to go before they have to start thinking about their Hall of Fame speeches. But as two of the best young quarterbacks in the NFL, it was important to tell the stories of their relationships with their fathers in *My First Coach*.

It was almost as if Carr had two fathers: Rodger, his real-life father; and his older brother David, his football father. The strength of Winston's relationship with his father, Antonor, was tested when Jameis had off-the-field troubles at Florida State. His father never stopped believing in him.

My First Coach is not just about the fathers who coached their sons on the field; rather, it's actually more about how they coached them off the field and taught them how to succeed in football and in life.

Sometimes, a dad just being a dad works out better than even the most supportive father could have planned. What can result in greatness? Athletic skill is required, of course, but supportive parents who can put their child in the best position to succeed are essential. But there are different formulas that work, as *My First Coach* illustrates. Often, there is even more frustration from the parents than the quarterbacks if they are not on the field.

Brady Sr. still holds a grudge against Michigan coach Lloyd Carr for the way he felt he mistreated Tom. Carr redshirted him his freshman year in 1995, then Tom threw only twenty passes as a backup over the next two years. The Wolverines won the national championship with Brian Griese at quarterback in '97, so it's hard to second-guess Carr's decision. Clearly, Brady was not yet the Brady who has won five Super Bowls.

Brady started all twenty-five games, putting together a 20-5 record, in his last two seasons at Michigan, but even so, Carr put Tom in a position where he was constantly forced to look over his shoulder at top prospect Drew Henson. Carr got Henson into seven games in 1998, often just for one series to give him experience and keep him happy. Carr began the 1999 season by having Brady play the first quarter, Henson play the second, and then decide at the half who would play the rest of the game. Eventually, he scrapped that rotation and Brady played all the time.

"All I hoped for is Tommy would get a chance to play in college," Tom Brady Sr. said. "Then I hoped he would get a chance to start. Then I hoped he would have a chance to get drafted in the pros and carry a clipboard for two to three years. To think he has reached the pinnacle of his world is beyond anybody's expectations, beyond anybody's dreams."

Brady has played for Bill Belichick, the best coach of this era. But the best coach of his life is also his hero and his best friend. His name is also Tom Brady. He was his first coach.

JIM HARBAUGH

Who's Got It Better Than Us?

Jack Harbaugh was sitting on the Colts bench at the old RCA Dome in downtown Indianapolis hours before kickoff of the final game of the 1994 season.

The dance team was on the field. Maybe fifteen people were in the stands. Jack, the head coach at Western Kentucky, had driven 265 miles on I-65 North to Indianapolis the previous evening from Bowling Green. His team's season was over, so this was a rare opportunity to see his son Jim play in person. After staying with Jim in his hotel room on Saturday night, they grabbed some breakfast with the team in the morning and then began the short walk to the stadium.

"Oh my God, I forgot my playbook," Jim said.

That was not surprising. "That's Jim Harbaugh," his dad said. "We had to make a U-turn, go back, and get his playbook."

They arrived at the stadium, and Jim went into the locker room to put on his warm-up gear. Jack waited for him on the bench. Jim had started at quarterback during the previous

13

week's victory against the Dolphins, but Browning Nagle was starting for the Colts that day against the Bills. The Colts were out of the play-offs, and they wanted to get a look at Nagle.

However, Nagle was awful and was benched after the first series of the third quarter and replaced by Harbaugh. It was a preview of the Captain Comeback nickname Jim earned the next season when he nearly completed a Hail Mary in the final seconds of the AFC Championship Game in Pittsburgh, a loss that kept him out of the Super Bowl. He threw a touchdown pass on his first series against the Bills and led the Colts to 10 points in the third quarter in their 10–9 victory, which was secured when Buffalo's Steve Christie hit the right upright with a 46-yard field goal attempt on the final play.

The game was not memorable. What happened before the game was a highlight in the lives of Jack and Jim Harbaugh. They each remember the moment's every detail.

Jim came out of the locker room and walked over to his father.

"Come on, Dad, play catch with me," he said. "I need somebody."

The offer brought tears to Jack's eyes then and even now. As he was tossing the ball back and forth with Jim from 10 yards away, he had a flashback. It took Jack back in time to Ann Arbor, Michigan, when he was an assistant coach on Bo Schembechler's staff. Jack would put in a full day of work preparing for the weekend's game, but he was able to come home to the house on Anderson Avenue for dinner after practice wrapped up. He lived fewer than two miles from campus. Back in the day, coaches had to wait for the old celluloid film to be developed by the team photographers before they could study what had transpired in practice. They were back in their office by 7 p.m., running the projector.

First came "the catch."

"I would be sitting in this chair, all tired," Jack said. "All I wanted to do was get dinner, read the paper or do whatever, and then go back to work. These two kids would come up to me and say, 'Hey, Dad, let's play catch.'"

John is exactly fifteen months older than little brother Jim. When Jack was in his first season at Michigan, John was eleven and Jim was ten. The boys had endless energy. Jack was only thirty-four years old and early in a coaching career that would span forty-six years. He loved playing catch with his boys when he wasn't tired, but knowing he would be returning to work after dinner and grinding until 11:30 p.m., and then having to do it all over again the next day, well, "Oh my God, the last thing I want to do is play catch," he said.

Often, with accuracy not necessarily a priority for his sons, it really wasn't catch at all.

"A lot of times it seems like I am chasing the ball," Jack said. "It was more chase than it is catch. I would crawl out of the chair and we would play catch for about twenty minutes."

Only then could he return to work.

Now he was helping Jim warm up on the sideline in Indianapolis before an NFL game. Jim was thirty-one years old. Jack was fifty-five. He thought about their catches in Ann Arbor and realized all that had really changed was that they were older now and the catch was in an NFL stadium. They had just taken their game of catch from the backyard to the big time. Imagine that.

"He had tears coming down," Jim said.

Jim recalled coming into the game early. He remembered he helped the Colts win the game. He kind of thought it was against the Bills, but he wasn't sure. "But I remember playing catch with my dad before the game," he said.

All these years later, Jim, too, gets emotional telling the story.

"Yeah," he said. "Just the power of catch."

Jim Harbaugh learned many things from his father that he has found to be useful as a father himself. He has seven children, three with his first wife, Miah, and four with his second wife, Sarah. His oldest child, Jay, is twenty-eight, and after working for his uncle John with the Ravens, he is Jim's running backs and assistant special teams coach at Michigan. His youngest child, John, was born on January 11, 2017.

Jim thinks back to the days in the backyard with his father and brother and to that precious day on the field in Indianapolis. He knows the lesson he will carry with him the rest of his life. "Play catch with your kids no matter how tired you are when you come home from work," he said. "That's a metaphor. You might be playing dolls, you might be climbing a tree, doing the things they want to do. Take them to things. Show them things. Take them to ball games. Most importantly, believe in them, because if you don't, who else is going to, and how else are they going to believe in themselves?"

||||||||||||||||||||||||||||||||||||||||||||

"Who's got it better than us? Noo-body."

Certainly nobody had it better than Jack Harbaugh the day he was down on the field at the RCA Dome playing catch with Jim.

The Harbaugh family slogan came to life on a hot-selling T-shirt at the M Den in Ann Arbor, where Jim Harbaugh has returned to his alma mater as head coach. He shouts the question in the Michigan locker room and his players enthusiastically answer. John Harbaugh, the coach of the Baltimore Ravens, has made it the motto in his locker room.

The football translation?

"You're really telling your team, 'I believe in you.' Who could have it better than us? Right?" Jim said. "What coaches could have it better? Then, when they say it back and answer, 'Nobody,' they're saying, 'We believe in you.' I learned that's part of self-talk. It's a tool you have; a weapon you have. It's not fake. Self-talk is a powerful tool that you have."

The first time the Harbaugh boys heard their father ask the question, it was 1971 and they were in Iowa City. Their dad was an assistant coach at the University of Iowa, and the Harbaughs were a one-car family. Jim was eight years old and John was nine. A local dealership provided each of the Iowa coaches with a loaner car, and one day Harbaugh's wife, Jackie, was using it. It was also a day the boys were off from school and Jack was taking them to work.

The university was two miles from the house, on the corner of Court Street. The three guys came out of the house.

"Hey, Dad, where's the car?" Jim asked.

"No car today, boys; we're walking," Jack said.

He had a plan.

"John, grab a basketball; Jim, grab a basketball. One hundred with the right. One hundred with the left. Here we go," Jack said.

They dribbled their way to the university's football office. Along the way, Jack introduced them to what was to become the family mantra.

"Who's got it better than us?" he asked.

"Nobody, Dad, nobody," they answered.

The boys would often ride their bicycles to Iowa's football practice, but boys being boys, they were a little rowdy, and Coach Frank Lauterbur decided no kids at practice anymore. Jack Harbaugh was upset. By the end of the season, he had been offered an assistant coaching job at Michigan. He accepted. Bo Schembechler allowed kids at practice. Bo didn't know it at the time, but little Jim Harbaugh would be his future quarterback.

Later, when Jim was coaching the 49ers, he went back to Iowa City to work out quarterback Ricky Stanzi before the 2011 draft. He had some time to kill after the meeting before he had to drive back to Cedar Rapids to catch a flight. He had two choices. He could grab something to eat. Or he could take a ride past the old house. He decided to take a trip down memory lane. He parked in front of the house he'd once called home, got out of the car, and took pictures.

"I remember thinking, 'This is the smallest house I have ever seen in my life,'" Jim said. "I remember when we lived there. It had a bedroom, and my mom, dad, and sister slept in that room. My brother and I shared a room. There was a kitchen. There was also the living room and a bathroom."

Jack would often walk into the boys' room at bedtime and tell them to keep it down. They did a lot of talking, and a lot of it was loud. Jack would come in once to quiet them down. He would come in twice. Still the volume didn't come down.

On the third trip, he gave up.

"Who could possibly have it better than you two?" he said. "You share, you laugh, you're brothers, you tell each other stories, you share your dreams. Who could have it better than you two?"

"Nobody, Dad, nobody."

Jim said, "We really thought we did. We really thought we had it better than anybody."

That memory was certainly better than Jim Harbaugh's initial introduction to his new hometown of Iowa City in March 1971 after his father was hired by the university.

"John and I had gone to school, our first day at Roosevelt Elementary," Jim once told the *Detroit Free Press*. "First day we'd moved there, found some kids to play with after school. It was getting dark. John said, 'We gotta go.' So we picked up our stuff and we're running. I was trying to put my jacket on over my head all at once. And I was just following after him and he crossed the street. Busy street there. The next thing I know, I woke up in a hospital bed. I'd got hit by a mail truck. Broke my leg in two places. Had a cast on for about six months. I was in the first grade. Second half of first grade."

Dan McGivern was the driver, and twenty years later, he realized that it was Jim Harbaugh, then the quarterback of the Chicago Bears, who was the kid from the accident. Harbaugh returned to his elementary school in Iowa City to speak to students. McGivern was sitting in the back of the classroom with other parents. Harbaugh was asked about the worst injury he had suffered and told the story of getting hit by a car.

McGivern, a twenty-year-old at the time of the accident, was driving a postal truck to help him pay his way through college at Iowa. Turns out, he was off duty at the time of the accident and driving his 1967 Ford Mustang on the way home when the accident occurred. He was still wearing his uniform, though.

"It was a really busy street, up a hill and on a flat section I see one kid run across so I'm aware," he told the *Detroit News*. "I look over and see another kid. He throws his coat up in the air like he was signaling touchdown, the coat comes over his head and he runs straight ahead. He's going to hit the front corner of my car. I swerve and he hit the right rear. He dented the back panel.

"I jumped out, took off my coat, and put it around him. Cars stopped. There was a lady with a baby carriage. She yelled to me, 'I saw the whole thing. It was not your fault.' The ambulance came. He's moaning a little bit. He tried to stand up, but his leg was off on a funny angle and I told him to stay down."

Dan visited Harbaugh in the hospital, and Jim's mother told him she knew the accident was not his fault.

After hearing that Harbaugh told the story on a radio show the week before Michigan played at Iowa in 2016, McGivern wrote Harbaugh a letter in January 2017 to let him know he was the driver. He asked for an autographed picture. Harbaugh called him and they spoke. One week later, Harbaugh was in Iowa City on a recruiting visit. He and McGivern met and reminisced. Harbaugh even posted a picture of the two of them along with McGivern's office phone number. "For comprehensive Life Insurance coverage, call Dan McGivern at..."

Who's got it better than us? Well...except for Jim back in the first grade.

The saying came to life in Crestline, Ohio, post–World War II. Jack Harbaugh grew up in a neighborhood filled with kids his age. His house was two doors down from the schoolyard. In the summertime, the kids would gather on the sandlot as the sun came up each morning. Rocks and cardboard sufficed as bases. They would play baseball until noon, take a lunch break, walk to one of their houses, enter through the back door, and the mom would make sandwiches for all of them. They would sit around a little bit, let their food digest, and then it was back to the baseball field for another game.

The boys would adjourn to their houses for dinner and get back together for a game of kick the can until it got dark at nine. They would get some sleep and do the same thing again the next day. It was nothing extravagant. Not some fancy sleep-away camp or day camp with in-ground swimming pools or picturesque lakes. Just a bunch of nine- and ten-year-olds entertaining themselves to pass the time in the summer heat.

One day, after coming to the conclusion that they did not have a care in the world except making sure they had enough kids to play a baseball game, one of the boys said, "Who's got it better than us?"

"Nobody," was the response.

Then it became, "Noo-body."

It was a routine they repeated two or three times a day.

"Somebody said, 'What an arrogant thing to feel,' that nobody had it better than us," Jack Harbaugh said.

It was a time of innocence. Nobody locked their houses. Kids didn't carry keys. If a family had a car, they left the key in the ignition. "No one had anything, so no one was going to steal anything," Jack said. "You had two pairs of pants and one was being washed. Everybody had it that way. One guy in town lived on a hill and actually had a riding lawn mower.

"We would stand next to that fence just looking and thinking, 'Wow, a riding lawn mower.' We were all in the same boat. We didn't have a lot, but we had each other. We were kidding each other, 'I'm going to be the shortstop of the Brooklyn Dodgers.'"

It was a talented group. Gates Brown actually went on to have a thirteen-year career with the Detroit Tigers. "He was in my class at school," Jack said. "He was one of the guys at the playground and part of the sandlot group." Two of Harbaugh's first cousins, Mike Gottfried and his brother Joe, showed up every day. Mike became a longtime college football coach, including head coaching stops at Murray State, Cincinnati, Kansas, and Pittsburgh. Joe was the head basketball coach at

Asheville College in Illinois, and later he was the athletic director at South Alabama.

Mike's nephew Mark, about the same age as Jim and John Harbaugh, was the head basketball coach at North Carolina State. One of Harbaugh's closest friends in the group was Dave Smith, a legendary sports editor in the golden age of newspapers who worked at the *Boston Globe* and the *Dallas Morning News*.

Jack played quarterback at Bowling Green and had a short stay in the old American Football League for one season in 1961. He began his coaching career three years later at a high school, and it became the family business with his sons following in his footsteps. His daughter, Joani, is married to Tom Crean, former Hoosiers basketball coach at Indiana University.

Once Jack had convinced his kids when they lived in Iowa City that nobody had it better than them, he faced another obstacle. The winters in Iowa. It was cold. The boys would be bundled up in their heavy coats, hats, gloves, and scarves. At least on those days they didn't have to walk to school.

"They looked like mummies getting out of the car," Jack said. "I'd never seen such sad guys in my whole life. They had frowns on their faces. They were all hunched over."

They were so unhappy, Jack said, they were almost crying.

"So, one day they are in the back seat and I turned around to them," he said. "They were just moseying out of the car again. [I said,] 'Come on, gentlemen, let's attack this day with an enthusiasm unknown to mankind. And don't take any wooden nickels.'"

Jim and John got out of the car without reacting. "That didn't make much of an impression," Jack said. "I did it the next day and the next day and the next day and the next day. I finally realized I was making no impression on them."

Now it's thirty-six years later, and Jack is watching Jim's introductory press conference as the head coach at Stanford University. Jim is asked how he is going to approach his first day on the job.

"We're going to attack this day with an enthusiasm unknown to mankind," Jim said. "And don't take any wooden nickels."

The smile that came across Jack's face could have lit up a room.

"My God, they were listening," he said.

Jack learned the saying from his father. No wooden nickels? What's the hidden meaning? "Don't let anybody sneak up from behind you and hit you over the head with a bag of crap," Jim said.

Lesson learned.

"Take no crap from anybody," Jack said. "I guess back in the days of streetcars they had these wooden nickels that they would put in the slot before they had modern technology."

||||||||||||||||||||||||||||||||||||||||||||

New Orleans was jumping for Super Bowl XLVII in February 2013. It was the first time the NFL had awarded the game to the Big Easy since Hurricane Katrina ripped apart the city in late August 2005. The Superdome was used as a shelter for nearly sixteen thousand people who could not evacuate before the hurricane blew through town with massive rain, relentless wind, and flooding when the levees failed.

The death toll eventually reached 1,833, including six people who died inside the Superdome. One man jumped fifty feet to his death in the massive stadium, claiming he had nothing left to live for as the Superdome became less a place of refuge and more like a prison. Urine in the hallways, feces everywhere, the smell unbearable. Part of the roof was destroyed, there was no electricity, and the heat was oppressive. The evacuees could not leave because of the rising water outside.

There was talk that the Saints would never return and could be on the move to San Antonio, where they had set up shop as New Orleans tried to recover. Commissioner Paul Tagliabue made sure that Saints owner Thomas Benson would not relocate the franchise to San Antonio, where he had many of his businesses, or anywhere else, even though they were unable to play in the Superdome in 2005. They returned home to play just thirteen months after Katrina and beat the Falcons on a festive evening in 2006.

Now it was seven and a half years later. In the famed French Quarter, the bars were hopping and the restaurants were packed. The Garden District, home to the Mannings, had escaped serious damage. In fact, walking around the French Quarter, there were no visible signs of the destruction that occurred in 2005. Music was blasting in the streets, half-naked women were disappearing and then reappearing on swings in and out of windows on Bourbon Street; and if you weren't paying attention, necklaces of beads being tossed by the half-naked women could hit you in the head.

There was human gridlock up and down the streets in the Quarter, not to mention plenty of Hurricanes—the kind you drink.

The Super Bowl was back in town. That was the story line for the first part of the week. As game day approached, Super Bowl XLVII became all about the Harbaugh Bowl. John, the coach of the Ravens, versus Jim, the coach of the 49ers. It should have been a dream for Jack and his wife, Jackie, but he believed in the parents' credo that you are only as happy as your unhappiest child. It was a given that either Jim or John would suffer the most devastating loss of his coaching career.

It was Jim's second year in San Francisco, after successful college stops at the University of San Diego and Stanford. John had been with the Ravens since 2008 after various college assistant jobs and his most recent stop as the Eagles special teams coach. John had been a defensive back at Miami of Ohio when Jim was Michigan's quarterback. It would be the first time in football, baseball, or basketball that brothers ever faced each other, as head coaches or managers, in the postseason.

John is a history buff, so he tried to put that game into perspective by saying, "It's not exactly Churchill and Roosevelt."

They were brothers, but they were different. Jim showed great reluctance in his press conferences to provide any in-depth information about his team and gave minimal insight into his relationship with John. But he sure did like to wear khaki pants every day with a black sweatshirt and sneakers. John was much more glib and frequently started off his answers by thanking reporters for their questions. If nothing else, the Harbaugh Bowl was unique; and it would likely be a very long time, if ever, before it was brother versus brother again in the Super Bowl. The NFL capitalized on the fact at their annual Friday morning press conferences with the coaches. Usually, the home team coach was up first, followed by a half-hour break and then the visiting team coach.

Always looking for ways to market the game, the NFL decided to have the Harbaughs conduct a press conference side by side. John was wearing a suit. Jim, of course, was attired in his trademark ensemble.

They were not only brothers, they were also very close. They shared a bedroom for sixteen years, in too many cities to remember, as their father worked his way up as a coach. They put tape across the middle of the room with the implied threat that if either crossed the line, trouble would ensue.

Who's got it better than them? Noo-body.

"We're not interesting," John said. "There is nothing more to learn. The tape across the middle of the room story. Okay, you got it? We're just like any other family. We get it. It's really cool and exciting and all that. It's really about the team, the players."

The truth is that if there had been a choice, it would have been much more comfortable for Jim to make the Super Bowl one year and John to make it the next or the other way around. It would have been easier on the coaches. It would have been easier on the family. Jim went so far as calling the Super Bowl matchup a "blessing and a curse. The blessing because it's my brother's team and also personally I played for the Ravens, worked with Ozzie Newsome and Art Modell. The curse part would be that talk of two brothers playing in the Super Bowl takes away from the players that are in the game."

The most poignant moment of the Friday press conference came when John was asked, as the older brother, whether it would be hard to take away a dream of Jim's to fulfill his own by winning the Super Bowl.

"No, not at all," John said. "I suspect he feels the same way. It's about the teams. We are fiercely loyal, there's no doubt. We all say that. Not just of one another—and we always have been. That's definitely not ever going to change; we will continue to be fiercely loyal and protective of one another, but also of our teams.

"Jim had mentioned earlier in the week...the band of brotherhood, the brothers that will take the field. That's true. The band of brothers will be the brothers on the sideline. It will be the Ravens' sideline, it will be the 49ers' sideline. That will be the band of brothers in this competition."

They were asked if they would ever hire the other onto their staff or work for their brother. They both said yes. John said he almost worked for Jim at Stanford. Jim's son Jay was the Ravens offensive quality control coach for Uncle John's Super Bowl team. Jim smiled when he mentioned that he heard his son was doing a phenomenal job. During the press conference, Jackie and Jack sat next to each other, proud of their sons but knowing it was going to be elation for one and misery for the other two days later.

The Ravens and the 49ers had met once previously in a regular season Harbaugh Bowl on Thanksgiving Night in 2011, with the Ravens winning 16–6 in Baltimore in a dreadful game that featured five field goals and only one touchdown. The Ravens had just 253 offensive yards and the 49ers had only 170. Jack and Jackie were in Baltimore for that game. Jackie was rooting for a tie. There could be no tie in the Super Bowl. She knew one of her sons was going to enjoy the ultimate victory while the other suffered the ultimate loss.

After that game in Baltimore, Jack went looking for his sons. He stuck his head in the Ravens locker room and saw the celebrating going on. He felt that Jim likely needed him more, and he went into the 49ers locker room and saw Jim standing by himself in the coaches' office. He realized that was where his presence would be more meaningful.

Once things settled down, John went out to the 49ers team bus to find his little brother. "It was just again the epitome of how everybody in the family feels about each other and always tries to raise one another up," Jackie Harbaugh said. "These are difficult times in football and everything when you're playing against your own brother. But at the end of the game, it's still about family and your feelings for one another."

Jack and Jackie Harbaugh knew that was a regular season game. By the next day, their sons would be focused on the next one. But this was the Super Bowl. There would be no next game the following week. Their stomachs were going to be tied up in knots on Super Bowl Sunday no matter who was winning, because it meant one of their sons was losing.

Archie Manning called Jack Harbaugh the Tuesday before the Super Bowl. The Harbaughs were already in New Orleans. Jack's cell phone rang. "Hi, this is Archie," Manning said. "I just want to tell you that Olivia and I are thinking about you. We're sitting here at the breakfast table and I know what you are going through."

Archie told Jack he hated it when his sons Peyton and Eli faced each other. Jack and Archie had never spoken before.

He framed the situation for Harbaugh perfectly. Sunday was not going to be an easy day. "The advice he gave us [was]: 'This will soon pass,'" Jack said. "I was looking for something a little more, not profound, because that's as profound as you can be. But I was looking for something in a little bit different [of a] direction."

Archie said that it was never Peyton versus Eli on the field at the same time, so he was just rooting for the offenses and he was rooting for the quarterback position.

"As a parent with two sons coaching, you've got to be thinking about the offense, defense, and special teams. There's so much more going through your mind watching games," Manning said.

"Interesting," Jack Harbaugh said.

Scary was what he really thought. Manning was able to get excited anytime either of his sons threw a touchdown pass. It would be different for Jack Harbaugh. If he cheered for a Ravens big play, that meant he was cheering against Jim and the 49ers. How was this going to work? If the 49ers intercepted

Joe Flacco and Jack got excited, did that mean he was rooting against John and the Ravens?

There was one other interesting phone call ten days prior to the Super Bowl. Jack and Jackie had been inundated with interview requests, so the decision was made to hold a national conference call to answer all the questions at once. It would save them a lot of time. The reporters identified themselves by name and affiliation and asked their questions.

"Question from Baltimore," the caller said. "Is it true that both of you like Jim better than John?"

Jackie started to answer, "We do not."

The caller sounded legitimate. But also sounded a lot like John. Before Jackie could go any further, her daughter, Joani, who had called in to listen, interrupted by saying, "Is that John?"

Then Jack said, "Is that John Harbaugh? Hey, John, Mom was ready to come right through this phone. I'm so happy that Joani recognized your voice."

John was amused. "You've got to keep the fighting spirit up," he said. "That's the way it should be, all right. That's all I needed to hear. I just needed to know that."

There was an ESPN story eighteen months after the Super Bowl that revealed part of the conversation the Harbaugh brothers had on the field before the game.

John grabbed Jim's wrist and hugged him. "I love you," John said. "Be good today."

"Okay," Jim said.

At the NFL owners meetings in March 2017 in Phoenix, John Harbaugh was walking down a hallway. He stopped for a moment when he was asked about expressing his love for Jim right before the biggest game of their lives.

He smiled.

"There was no brotherly love at that moment," he said. "It was all brotherly competition."

What did they talk about?

"We talked about nothing." John laughed. "We talked about the kicker. He said I was harassing his kicker because I was talking with David Akers, who I had coached with Andy [Reid in Philadelphia] for all those years."

They did take time to acknowledge the unique place in history they now held as the only brothers to face each other as head coaches in the Super Bowl. It may never happen again. "We did kind of say it's pretty cool and pretty amazing," John said.

Did one say to the other, "I want to kick your ass"?

"That was unspoken," John said.

It turned into one of the wildest Super Bowls of all time. The Ravens were dominating until 13:22 remained in the third quarter. They held a 28–6 lead. It was almost going to be better this way for the Harbaugh parents. A crushing close loss would make consoling the loser that much more difficult. But a lopsided loss could be forgotten quicker as just one of those days.

Then the lights inside half of the Superdome went out. From one second to the next, half the stadium went dark. It happened just two plays after Jacoby Jones returned the second-half kickoff 108 yards for the Ravens, the longest play in Super Bowl history. The lights went out for twenty-five minutes, causing a thirty-four-minute delay. It was just what the 49ers needed. They took a deep breath, regrouped, and when the lights came back on they scored the next 17 points to get to 28–23.

Game on.

The 49ers were down 34–29 when they reached the Baltimore 7-yard line with 2:39 left. There were some awfully anxious Harbaughs in the stadium. The game was going to come down to the final play. They knew the television cameras would be on them, waiting for a reaction.

"If you scratch your head or you raise your hand, there's an appearance that you might favor one over the other," Jack Harbaugh said. "So you were like a zombie. We just sat stone-faced for fear the camera would catch you with a smile on your face. Whatever was going on in the game, the perception was you might favor one over the other."

San Francisco's furious comeback came down to this: Could Jim Harbaugh, a state-of-the-art offensive coach, dial up a winner to produce a touchdown to beat his brother, John, in the Super Bowl?

LaMichael James ran for 2 yards on first down. Colin Kaepernick threw an incomplete pass to Michael Crabtree. Now it was third and goal at the 5. Kaepernick once again tried to get the ball to Crabtree, who briefly had it before Jimmy Smith knocked it loose at the 3. Jim Harbaugh was calling for pass interference. All flags stayed in the pockets of the seven officials.

One play for the Harbaugh Bowl. "I'd prefer it be called the Super Bowl," Jackie Harbaugh said.

Kaepernick audibled at the line after taking a look at the Ravens defense and was pressured as he released a fade pass to Crabtree in the right corner of the end zone. It was close as to whether Smith was holding Crabtree, but once again, no flag. Jim Harbaugh was extremely upset at the non-call.

"I really want to handle this with class and grace," he said. "We had several opportunities and didn't make enough plays. Yes, there was no question in my mind there was a pass interference and then a hold on Crabtree on the last one. In my opinion, the drive should have continued."

The Ravens regained possession at their 5-yard line with 1:46 remaining. John Harbaugh ordered his punter to take an intentional safety with twelve seconds remaining that made the score 34–31. The clock ran out when Ted Ginn returned the free kick to the 50.

John, the winning coach, and Jim, the losing coach, met at midfield. It was the most difficult postgame get-together of John's career. He was elated for himself and his team. He was heartbroken for his brother.

"I felt bad for my brother, but not as bad as I would have felt for myself if we had lost," John said.

John intended to give his brother a hug. Jim stuck out his arm to block him from moving in.

"There will be no hug," Jim said.

John thought Jim called "an amazing game. It was incredible the way they came back," but when asked if his younger brother felt pressure and made mistakes on the final few play calls because he wanted so badly to beat him, he said, "No way. I love his creativity. I thought it was masterful what they did."

Jim put his hand on John's cheek and John slapped his brother twice on the chest. John told Jim he loved him. Jim told John he was proud of him. Jack and Jackie first met with Jim to console him. Then they made their way over to John. "How is Jim?" was the first thing John asked.

Jack and Jackie left the Superdome. They didn't go to the Ravens victory party. They did not go to the 49ers' hotel for their postseason party either. They just walked around New Orleans for forty-five minutes talking. Tom Crean, their son-in-law, told Jack that Doc Rivers—Crean had coached at Marquette years after Rivers played there—had said to him, "I can only imagine how your in-laws feel."

There was no celebration for the parents of the Super Bowl coaches. Elation for one Harbaugh coach. Heartbreak for the other. Right down the middle for Jack and Jackie. "We found a place that was open late and we went in and had some food and refreshment," Jack said.

"Then we went to our rooms. That was the evening."

Jim has heard his father talk about how a parent can be only as happy as their least happy child. That would be Jack Harbaugh on this extraordinary night in New Orleans. "It was fair, healthy, honest competition at the very highest level and we were both there," Jim said. "I'm very proud of my brother. Very happy for him."

The game had a deep impact on the Harbaugh family. It was

historical. John said he "couldn't measure" the effect the game has had on their lives and their relationship. Now that Jim is not coaching in the NFL, he shows up on the Ravens sideline when he has a break in his schedule. John has been very supportive of Jim's efforts at Michigan.

"I think he's the best coach in football," John said.

||||||||||||||||||||||||||||||||||||||||||||

Jim Harbaugh's corner office in Schembechler Hall on State Street in Ann Arbor looks right into the massive indoor practice facility for the University of Michigan Wolverines. After two NFC Championship Game appearances and a Super Bowl loss in his first four years in San Francisco, Jim had a falling-out with 49ers owner Jed York and general manager Trent Baalke and was fired after the 2014 season.

Harbaugh was unemployed for less time than it used to take Mike Ditka to scream at him for throwing a bad interception when he was the quarterback of the Chicago Bears. Michigan wanted Harbaugh to come back to his alma mater to replace Rich Rodriguez in 2011, but when he decided to leave Stanford, he chose the 49ers over Michigan, the Dolphins, the Raiders, and the Broncos. He was able to keep his family in the same house in the Bay Area.

In just his second season at Michigan in 2016, Jim had his school in contention for the national title until a crushing late-season overtime loss at archrival Ohio State. Twenty years earlier, as a senior, he had guaranteed that Michigan would beat

Ohio State to earn a trip to the Rose Bowl. He created a lot of controversy, but he followed through on his guarantee.

Harbaugh soon became a lightning rod in college football with his satellite camps/recruiting junkets for high school kids. He incurred the wrath of Alabama coach Nick Saban and others, but Harbaugh cared about only one thing: getting the best players to attend Michigan.

Jim's decision to accept Michigan's offer was great for his family. His kids enrolled at St. Francis of Assisi, the same elementary school Harbaugh attended when his father worked for Bo. His parents had been living in Milwaukee. After Jack retired from coaching in 2002, he took an associate athletic director's job at Marquette a few years after Crean was hired to coach the basketball team. Of course, not only wasn't it enough that his sons followed him into coaching, but his daughter married a basketball coach.

"The interesting thing is, [with] what I know about basketball and what my wife knows about basketball, we could not blow up a small balloon," Jack said. "Now we have to at least learn a few buzzwords so we feel we can carry on a conversation with him."

Joani met Crean at Western Kentucky when Jack was the head football coach. Crean was on the basketball staff as an assistant to Ralph Willard. When Willard was hired by Pitt, Crean went with him. Crean and Tom Izzo had once been graduate assistants at Michigan State under Jud Heathcote—Magic Johnson's coach—and when Izzo was hired to replace him in 1995, Crean went along as his assistant.

"They kind of had a pact that whoever got the first head coaching job, the other guy would come and work with him," Jack Harbaugh said. "So he left Pitt and went to Michigan State and then on to Marquette."

Once Crean and Joani had moved on to Indiana in 2008, there was nothing keeping the Harbaughs in Milwaukee. They packed up their house in June 2016 and relocated to Ann Arbor, right around the corner from Jim and his family. Jack and Jackie live on Aberdeen Drive in a house that had been empty for a couple of years. Jim and Sarah live on Arlington Boulevard, five doors down from where Schembechler used to live. Every morning, Jack stands in front of his house as three of his grandchildren come running over the hill to say good morning before they head off to school.

"As we say in the Harbaugh family, 'Who's got it better than us?' Literally nobody," Jack said.

Jim Harbaugh was the first-round draft pick of the Chicago Bears in 1987 after an excellent career playing quarterback for Schembechler, who out-recruited Western Michigan's Jack Harbaugh to get the signature on a letter of intent for one of the hottest high school quarterback prospects in the country.

Jack was an assistant coach for seven years at Michigan, and Jim played there for four years. But Jack was never able to enjoy the amazing spectacle of a college football Saturday in the Big House. He was too busy as a coach and was able to watch his son play only once at Michigan Stadium. In Jim's first season back as the head coach, Jack and Jackie were still living in Milwaukee. But they made sure they were in town for Jim's first home game against Oregon State.

It was surreal. He coached at Michigan. His son played at Michigan. Now Jack was retired and his son was the head coach at Michigan. "I'm watching the band play the fight song coming down the field," Jack said. "I got the hair on the back of my neck standing straight up. When I was coaching there, right before the game, you would go into the press box. They didn't have elevators in those days and you would have to come through the stands." At halftime, the assistant coaches made their way through the stands to get to the locker room to help Schembechler with adjustments.

Harbaugh now was a fan with a special connection to the head coach. Now he understood why a college football Saturday in Ann Arbor, with the students treating game day like their Mardi Gras, was so special. "I was here seven years and missed all this," he said. "I would have loved to have been part of the whole Michigan experience. I had this day job and couldn't really enjoy this as much as I am now. It is a fantastic experience for Jackie and myself."

Jack was able to see Jim play in person just three times total during his college career. Jackie made it to every home game. "I would be at Western Michigan coaching a game and I would have these headsets on," Jack said. "I know Jim is playing at Michigan and I'm wondering what is going on over there. The stadium announcer says, 'Now we have a score from Ann Arbor, Michigan.' I would loosen my headsets and hear the score. I would get an idea how the game was going and how things might be going for Jim."

Jim and Jack are able to share football. Every day, Jim says, he wants to make his father proud. Jack sits in the stands at the Big House for games now that Jim is coaching, but prior to the game he's down on the field with Jim. "A big motivator is my dad," Jim said. "He is to this day. He's said it before and I've heard him say it: 'The game was first played in 1868. There are no motivational tricks left. They've all been found and used.' He prefers to go with the truth. What other powerful motivator is there?"

Jack just couldn't convince Jim to come play for him at Western Michigan. He had been at Stanford as the defensive coordinator when Jim was a senior at Palo Alto High School. Jack once picked up a recruit at the airport on a Friday afternoon and detoured to watch Jim play in a basketball game before taking the high school kid to see the Stanford campus. As Jim was narrowing down his choices of where to attend college, Jack was hired by Western Michigan for his first head coaching job. He knew who he wanted as his quarterback, but he didn't want to push too hard.

"We're having a conversation. My mom was on one phone; I was on the other. My dad was in Kalamazoo, so we were having this three-way conversation. So we all three could talk and try to decide where I'm going to go," Jim said. "I hadn't got the scholarship offer to Michigan yet. We'd kind of come to the conclusion, if Michigan offers me a scholarship, that's where I'm going to go. That's the gist of the conversation. That's where you should go."

"If you go to Michigan, it's the best program. You play for Bo Schembechler. You'd be an All-American there. You could win the Heisman Trophy at Michigan," Jack said.

His dad had finished talking. He was going to Michigan if they offered.

There was a pause.

"Hang up, Jim. I want to talk to your mom," Jack said.

"Okay," Jim said.

He was about to put down the phone but couldn't help himself. He listened in.

His parents talked about Wisconsin. They talked about Arizona.

"You know what I want him to do?" Jack said.

"What?" Jackie said.

"I want him to go to Western Michigan. I want to coach him," Jack said.

Jim was not supposed to hear that. "I started thinking if Michigan doesn't offer me, I'll go to Western Michigan and play for my dad. That would be awesome," Jim said.

He went on his official visit to Michigan two days later. Before Jim arrived, Schembechler called Jack in Kalamazoo and told him his son would be visiting for forty-eight hours. "Here's what we are going to do. After forty-eight hours, we are going to send him over to Kalamazoo and you got one day with him," Schembechler said. "You can talk him into coming with you. I totally understand. But you got twenty-four hours."

By the end of the weekend, nine years after nine-year-old Jim Harbaugh sat in Schembechler's chair in his office when his father was an assistant, the iconic coach offered him a scholarship to play at the University of Michigan.

"I suppose that's a full scholarship," Jim said.

Bo laughed. Yes, it was. Jim accepted. "Well, I'm coming to Michigan then," he said.

He paid a courtesy visit to his dad. They both knew it was in his best interests to play at Michigan and not at Western Michigan. Jim was redshirted as a freshman and spent five years at Michigan. His father was fired after five years at Western Michigan with a 26-26-3 record.

"I have a strong, strong feeling that my experience at Western Michigan would have been a lot better and I would have ended up keeping my job there if I had him," Jack said. "It was a lot more than just being around him and having a chance to coach him. My whole coaching career might have turned out differently."

Jack didn't have an up-close view to see how hard his friend Bo coached Jim. But years later, after Jim was in Chicago, he became the favorite whipping boy of volatile coach Mike Ditka. It could not have been easy to watch Ditka verbally abuse Jim in a 1992 game at Minnesota. The Bears led 20–0 going into the fourth quarter. Harbaugh audibled out of a play sent to him from the sidelines and threw an interception that was returned for a touchdown. Ditka got in Harbaugh's face as he came to the sidelines. It started the Vikings on the way to a 21–20 victory.

"Sometimes, we get too smart for our own selves," Ditka said after the game. "When the player knows more than the coach, you have a problem. I'm not going to put forty-seven guys' careers in the hand of somebody who thinks he knows more than I know."

What did that mean?

"Can't call an audible anymore," Harbaugh said. "He's the coach."

Harbaugh had been conditioned to being yelled at by Schembechler, who was animated on the sidelines. Jim often frustrated Bo. "You will never play another down for me as long as you are here!" Bo screamed more than once at Harbaugh.

Jack Harbaugh was in his fourth year of coaching Western Kentucky. He was sitting at home in Bowling Green watching the Vikings-Bears game. On the television screen in front of him, Ditka was blistering his son. "When he threw the ball, I kind of had the reaction, 'This is not good. Something is going to happen,'" Jack said. "Then he started in on him. You just felt so badly for him. How do you react? I thought Jim handled it perfectly. He didn't walk away. He didn't respond in any way. He just looked him in the eye. Ditka walked away a couple of times; he came back and Jim looked him right in the eye. I was proud of him that he was man enough to handle it about as well as you possibly could."

Jack Harbaugh retired from coaching after nearly five decades following the 2002 season at Western Kentucky. He relocated to Milwaukee to be close to Joani and Tom Crean and their children, and accepted a job at Marquette. Two years later, Jim was hired for his first head coaching job at the University of San Diego after he began his coaching career with two years as the Raiders quarterbacks coach. Jim asked Jack to help out that season with the running backs. Jack took a leave of absence from Marquette for a nonpaying job working for his son, and he and Jackie were off to California.

Jack returned to Marquette after the season. Jim and John had helped him during his coaching career, and he felt good about returning the favor. Five years later, Jim called again. Willie Taggart, his running backs coach at Stanford, accepted a job as the head coach at Western Kentucky. Stanford was getting ready to play in the Sun Bowl, and Harbaugh gave Taggart permission to leave early so he could recruit and get the program in order. Jim didn't want to spend time looking for a new assistant coach while he was preparing for a bowl game, so he called his father.

"He asked me if I would come and work for three weeks and then I would be off in the sunset," Jack said. "I said, 'I'd love to.'"

Toby Gerhart, who would go on to play in the NFL, was Stanford's featured running back and a Heisman finalist. Jack Harbaugh called Gerhart over for a talk after the first practice.

"Maybe you and I can take a walk," Harbaugh said.

Gerhart had a serious look on his face. He had no idea what the coach's father wanted to talk to him about.

"Toby, here is the deal: I am not the running back coach at Stanford University and I have no ambition of this being my job. I'm not auditioning for this job. Really, I'm past that time. This will be the only game I will be coaching," he said.

Gerhart still didn't know what was going on.

"I have a favor to ask of you," Harbaugh said.

"Yeah, Coach," Gerhart said.

"My goal for the next three weeks in preparation for the game in the Sun Bowl is not to get yelled at by the head coach. You know there is no one who will not get yelled at by the head coach if he deems it necessary," Harbaugh said.

He set the agenda: No fumbles; no missed blitz pickups; block your man.

"If you can go four weeks and you can do that and I don't get yelled at by the head coach, I'm going to consider this one of the great experiences of my life," Harbaugh said.

Gerhart had a big smile on his face. He had led the nation with 1,736 yards rushing. He carried the ball 32 times for 135 yards and two touchdowns in the Sun Bowl, but the Cardinal lost to Oklahoma, 31–27. Gerhart did not fumble. Stanford allowed just one sack.

Jack Harbaugh has always been Jim Harbaugh's go-to guy. The family moved around the country as Jack moved up the ranks in coaching, but they always had one another. The kids made friends all over the country. Just when they became entrenched in the community, Jack got a new job and it was time to pack up. One time, when they were living in Iowa, Jim was ready to move before Jack.

"Do you have any job offers?" Jim asked when he came home from school one day.

"No, I really don't," Jack said.

"You better get one, because today I lost my last friend. It's time for us to move again," Jim said.

Jim had that kind of personality. He was so intense, so

competitive, he could wear out his friends. It's no different now that he's coaching. He wants things done his way. That's why his stay in San Francisco lasted only four years despite tremendous success and when the 49ers were thinking they had the next Bill Walsh. That's why he's in the perfect spot back in Ann Arbor. He spent seven years there as a kid, the longest stop for the traveling Harbaugh family, and then five more years as a student at Michigan.

Jack loves that Jim has returned to the scene of some of the happiest days of his own coaching career. He now attends games as the patriarch of the football program. He stops by the football office daily, even if Jim is out of town. He loves being at receptions with the guys he coached with under Schembechler and with his former players.

"It's unbelievable," he said.

Jim still leans on Jack for advice, and when his father tells him that a play or a philosophy worked for him in 1989 at Western Kentucky, Jim responds, "Perfect, I'm going to do it exactly the same way."

Jim says, "I save myself a three-hour migraine and I have the right answer in a minute and a half."

In the Harbaugh household, there was never any doubt that Father knew best.

Who's got it better?

ELI MANNING

The First Family of Football

Ninth grader Eli Manning was the starting junior varsity quarterback and the backup varsity quarterback at Isidore Newman High School, a private prep school located on eleven acres in the Uptown section of New Orleans. It was strong in academics and strong in athletics.

His two brothers had also attended Newman. Cooper, seven years older, was a receiver; and Peyton, five years older, was a quarterback. Peyton-to-Cooper in Cooper's senior season was one of the most prolific high school quarterback-receiver combinations in the country.

The Manning boys were as different as three boys could be. Cooper was the comedian. Peyton was controlling. Eli was easygoing.

Sometimes, Eli was so easygoing even his parents wondered if he had a pulse. Like the day he started his first varsity game.

Frank Gendusa, the Newman football coach, suspended starting quarterback Cole LeBourgeois one game for a violation of a team rule. Eli had known for days he was going to start the next game. He knew it was just a one-time deal until he took over as the starter his sophomore year.

Even so, it was pretty big news in the Manning house to everyone except Eli.

He was sitting at the dinner table with his parents, Archie and Olivia, the night before the game.

"You going to be there?" Eli asked.

"Sure we're going to be there," Archie said.

"I'm starting," Eli said.

"What?" Archie said.

"Yeah, Cole got suspended," Eli said.

"When did you find out? Yesterday?" Archie said.

"No, he got suspended over the weekend," Eli said.

Manning practiced Monday, Tuesday, and Wednesday as the starter but never told his father, the former quarterback at Ole Miss, the New Orleans Saints, the Houston Oilers, and the Minnesota Vikings.

Most of Newman's games were played on Friday nights. This one was on Thursday night, which happened to be the night of Eli's favorite television show. The football players always remained at Newman to hang out after class and didn't come home before the 7:30 p.m. kickoff.

The phone rang in the Mannings' Garden District home at 5:30. It was just two hours until game time. Olivia picked up.

"Mom," Eli said.

"What's wrong?" Olivia asked.

"Mom, can you tape *Seinfeld* for me?" Eli said.

He was about to start his first high school game and was more concerned about Jerry, Elaine, George, and Kramer. The Thursday night game had thrown off his television timing, and he'd forgotten to set the VCR at home.

Manning then went out and completed 5 of 8 passes for 90 yards and a touchdown in a victory over rival Fisher High School.

Well, that's how Archie tells the story.

Eli is a dedicated *Seinfeld* fan, but he thinks his father is confusing things a bit. His memory is that the *"Seinfeld"* game occurred in his sophomore or junior year. "Different stories mixed into one. Possibly. But that happens." Eli laughed. "Go with my dad's story; it sounds better."

True to his nickname, "Easy" never lets them see him sweat. Whether it was indeed his first start or a game later in his high school career or his first start in the NFL or his first start in a Super Bowl, he gets more excited pulling off one of his many practical jokes on teammates than he does for a game. Nothing bothers him. Nothing makes him nervous except possibly missing *Seinfeld* reruns. He is still a big fan.

Although Eli didn't eclipse Peyton's high school record for passing yards, the three Manning brothers brought national prominence to Newman. Many years later, another Newman alum joined Manning with the Giants: wide receiver Odell Beckham Jr.

||||||||||||||||||||||||||||||||||||||||||||||||||

The oldest child gets smothered with attention because that's what happens with first-time parents. The middle child is often low-maintenance and the one who feels neglected, with so much of the parents' time spent on the new issues being encountered by the oldest and the extra attention required by the youngest.

The youngest one gets dragged along to the activities of the older siblings, which can make them enthusiastic to participate or be a turnoff and steer them in a different direction. Eli was dragged to plenty of his brothers' games.

"Eli has been extremely supportive of me at all my sporting events, going way back," Peyton said. "Eli had to go to a lot of them just due to my parents not having a babysitter all the time. Eli is like, 'I guess I have to go to the game.' Baseball games, basketball games. He's seen me play a lot, but I've always made a point to watch Eli play one time a season when he was in high school; my bye week when I was in college and then when I was in the pros, my bye week I'd always go see Ole Miss play. And certainly watched the Giants whenever I had a chance. Nobody pulls harder for Eli than I do."

When Eli was born in 1981, he was treated like a typical third child. Cooper and Peyton were into all the sports, and Eli had to come along for the ride. When he was old enough to understand what was going on, he knew enough that it wasn't much fun watching his brothers play.

Cooper and Peyton were almost exactly two years apart and did a lot together.

"When you are ten, eight, and three, that's a big gap," Archie said. "Eli was so much younger. You just drag him along. The older boys were really active. There were a lot of Little League baseball games, there were a lot of gymnasiums playing in basketball leagues, and then you have a three-year-old. I always told Olivia, 'This child is not going to like sports because his brothers like playing everything.' He finally started asking us to get him a babysitter."

Eli had to tag along when his brothers played baseball on Saturdays and Sundays. If they advanced to the second day of a tournament, the Mannings would show up at the field not knowing if they were going to be watching one game or six games. If they kept winning, they kept playing and Eli kept watching. Or was forced to watch. "Poor old Eli," Archie said. "This child is going to have other interests besides athletics."

Archie Manning had developed very close relationships with Cooper and Peyton before Eli was born. He naturally wanted the same with Eli. He had his own career with the Saints, but with the family living in New Orleans, he had plenty of time for his kids. Once the Saints broke their six-week training camp in Mississippi, Florida, or Louisiana—the team bounced around quite a bit—Archie was home for the season. Of course, there were the overnight trips to road games, and the family made a big deal of the few times they would pick Dad up at the airport on Sunday nights, which helped raise his spirits with the Saints invariably coming home after another losing effort.

Archie would usually drive himself to what is now called Louis Armstrong New Orleans International Airport to get to the team plane, but one Saturday he hitched a ride with a teammate. This was before Eli was even born. Olivia took Cooper and Peyton with her to pick him up on Sunday night. Archie was down in the dumps. He had played poorly and the Saints lost.

"Hey, guys, what did you think about the game?" Archie said when he got in the car.

He was expecting to hear, "Dad, you were great," or, "We'll do better next week."

Not a chance.

"Oh, we watched the Dolphins today," Cooper said.

Archie couldn't help but crack up. "He was just trying to make me laugh," he said. "He's still like that."

As Eli got older, he followed the same path as Cooper and Peyton. He wanted to play everything. When he was ten, he played in the same Little League in New Orleans that his older brothers had played in. He played high school football at Newman, the same school as his brothers. There was one significant difference, though.

"Eli was very shy and quiet," Archie said.

Archie was sensitive to Eli's personality and needs. He always wanted to have the same enthusiasm for his third son as he had for his first two. Eli was going down the same path as Cooper and Peyton, and that meant Archie was going down the same path for the third time in seven years. As Eli grew older, his brothers would invite him on weekends in the off-season to join them at the high school to work out with their teammates and friends. He would run routes, play a little quarterback, play some linebacker, play cornerback.

"I always felt included," he said. "I was just out there, happy to be along. When you're ten years old and you're hanging out with the high school football team and some of the players, that's cool. That's what you want to do."

He didn't care about getting reps at quarterback or how much the older guys would let him play. He was just a kid. "You just didn't want to make a mistake," he said. "You just wanted to feel involved."

When his brothers graduated high school and Eli was learning how to play quarterback, he would go to the same football field with Archie. "When I wanted somebody to run routes for me, he would," Eli said. "By the time I got there, he really couldn't run the routes anymore. His knees were starting to fail on him. He could still run the tail end of a route. He could still be there to help."

Archie never pushed his sons to play football. He never encouraged Peyton and Eli to be quarterbacks. He never imagined they would win four Super Bowls between them, including back-to-back Super Bowl XLI, when the Colts beat the Bears, and Super Bowl XLII, when the Giants beat the Patriots. He wanted them to find their own way. He was there to guide them. Even though he was certainly qualified and must have been tempted, Archie didn't coach his kids in football.

"I don't think it was a situation where he was telling me reads or telling me how to practice or how to play the game," Eli said. "We never really got into it. He really let our coaches do the coaching and for us to try and enjoy our high school experience. That's the way he enjoyed his high school experience.

He wanted us to do the same thing. He never got involved or tried to be a coach. He wasn't the guy coming to practice and watching us practice every day. He was doing his deal. We were doing our deal."

Eli became Newman's starting quarterback in his sophomore season. By then, Peyton was well-established at Tennessee, but Cooper was forced to give up football before he even stepped on the field as a freshman at Mississippi, his father's school. He was experiencing numbness in his hand during preseason practices. He went to the Mayo Clinic in Rochester, Minnesota, and was diagnosed with spinal stenosis, a narrowing of the spinal column. One bad hit and he could be paralyzed. He underwent a difficult surgery and his football career was over. Eli was just eleven. Peyton was sixteen and already a hot college prospect. Peyton took the news about Cooper especially hard.

Cooper then wrote a heartbreaking and heartfelt letter to Peyton.

"I would like to live my dream of playing football through you," he wrote. "Although I cannot play anymore, I know I can still get the same feeling out of watching my little brother do what he does best. I know now that we are good for each other, because I need you to be serious and look at things from a different perspective. I am good for you, as well, to take things light. I love you, Peyt, and only great things lie ahead for you. Thanks for everything on and off the field."

Eli was too young for Cooper to even be thinking about his youngest brother's potential athletic accomplishments. Eli first had to figure things out in school. He had enrolled at Newman, but he was having issues in the first grade. On the playground, he was active and coordinated. He was also taller than the other kids. But he was having trouble in the classroom.

"He wasn't reading well," Archie said. "He wasn't keeping up. Newman is pretty hard."

The school's counselors contacted the Mannings. They were going to hold Eli back and make him repeat first grade.

"Olivia and I thought that would really socially affect him," Archie said. "They might read better than him, but on the playground and so forth, he would have gone back with kids who seemed so much smaller than him. So we transferred."

Eli enrolled at St. George's, a small school that he has since supported financially. "He has never forgotten what that school did for him," Archie said. "It's a wonderful little school. Eli has been very generous to them since he's been in professional football, with his money and some time."

St. George's didn't make Eli repeat first grade. He went into the second grade, and they had a reading program that gave him extra help. He made new friends and caught up with his reading. The school went through the eighth grade, and Archie wanted Eli to graduate from St. George's before deciding where to go to high school. Eli was ready to return to Newman. Cooper and Peyton had graduated from Newman, and now that academics were no longer an issue, Eli felt it was the right place for him.

"Newman is very challenging academically," Archie said. "I never wanted my children to be stressed about academics. Do your best, but we won't stress on that."

Eli insisted. He wanted to go back to Newman. He wanted

to play football at Newman. "There are plenty of other good schools here," Archie told him.

Not only did he want to go back to Newman, but Eli wanted to enroll in the eighth grade there rather than graduate St. George's. To prevent high school athletic recruiting, if a student was at Newman in the eighth grade, he could play high school sports in the ninth grade. But if he was coming from another school after graduating the eighth grade and didn't enroll until the ninth grade, he couldn't play until tenth grade.

Eli got his way with his parents. "He never had a problem," Archie said. "Eli wound up being an academic All-American."

Even when he was at St. George's, Eli spent a lot of time over at Newman. "I went to watch the basketball games," he said. "A lot of my buddies were still at the school. I played other sports with them. I played baseball and basketball with them in different leagues. I eventually wanted to go back to Newman. Once I got the reading figured out—I had some difficulty with it, and it just took a little longer—I probably could have gone to Newman earlier."

One athletic advantage to remaining at St. George's: They played flag football beginning in the fifth grade. "I enjoyed doing that," he said. "So I stayed and went back to Newman in the eighth grade."

||||||||||||||||||||||||||||||||||||||||||||

Archie Manning was traded during the 1982 season to the Houston Oilers by the Saints. The Saints had drafted him in the first round in 1971, and he was raising a family in the Big Easy. Eli was not even two yet, and Archie had to pack up in the middle of the season to play in Texas. The family remained behind in New Orleans. This was not ideal.

Manning was a terrific quarterback who had the misfortune to play on miserable teams. Archie is the best quarterback in NFL history to never appear in the play-offs. The Saints were historically bad. They narrowly escaped becoming the first team to finish a season 0-16 when they defeated the New York Jets in the fifteenth game of the 1980 season.

Despite all the losing, professional football was a good life for Archie. He was always there for Olivia and the kids. Then he wasn't. He was off to Houston, and then during the 1983 season he was traded to the Vikings, too far away in Minneapolis.

"I spent more than a year up there by myself," he said.

He retired after the 1984 season. One of the reasons was Eli.

"I sensed that my relationship wasn't quite the same with Eli that it had been with Cooper and Peyton at that age," he said. "Eli was kind of shy anyway, and it might have been a little harder for Eli to warm up to you. I was gone and I didn't like it at all. I remember that was one of the real joys for me when I retired that I would be home, that I would be around full-time for Eli, get that relationship that I had with Cooper and Peyton because it was a good one."

Archie knew that being around his family was what worked for him as a dad. The travel schedules for professional athletes in baseball, basketball, and hockey are brutal, and some football players might even choose to live away from their families during the season, but Manning wanted to be home. He turned down opportunities right after he retired to enter the broadcasting business so he could be around his family full-time.

"I knew it wasn't going to be long after I quit playing that my kids were going to be playing on Saturday mornings, junior high, JV, and eventually Friday nights," he said. "I didn't want to miss that. I just didn't. It wasn't because I was going to be there to coach them. I just wanted to be there."

He was not being a helicopter parent. He was being an engaged parent. His kids didn't need Archie to prove that he cared. If his kids were playing in a game, he didn't feel obligated to be there; he went because he wanted to see them play and be there for them.

"I'm not saying that is the only way to go and you have to do that to have a father-son relationship; I'm just saying that is what I wanted to do," he said. "I'm sure losing my dad influenced my thinking in some way."

Archie was nearly twenty years old in 1969 when his father, Buddy, committed suicide. Archie was home for the summer after his sophomore year at Ole Miss. The older man suffered from health and business problems and was a heavy smoker. Archie came home late one afternoon after attending a wedding and discovered his father's motionless body on his bed with a bullet hole through his chest.

"He was stubborn," Manning told ESPN. "He was tough. He had a stroke and he didn't go to the doctor for two weeks. He smoked, like everybody. Smoked Chesterfields. He wore to work, every day, a pair of khakis and a shirt. And he had to have two front pockets. If you gave him a birthday present, and it had one front pocket, it was never going to come out of the wrapper. One pocket for his pens and one for his Chesterfields."

Archie and Buddy were very close, and losing him like that, and being the one to discover the body, had a profound impact on Archie's desire to be around his three sons as much as possible.

"I wish I'd had my dad a lot longer. He was part of my life and had great influence on me," he said. "I wish I'd had him more. I think when something like that happens—that it had a lot to do with me just really wanting to be around."

Manning considers it a bonus that his sons were great athletes. His goal was for them to be good kids and love one another, be one another's best friends, take care of one another. He never put pressure on them to be football players, to follow him as a quarterback. He would play "Amazing Catches" with them in the yard, during which he was the quarterback and the boys all wanted Archie to make them stretch out to make an amazing catch. Those were the most intense games he ever played with them.

"They would start at one end of the yard and take off," Archie said. "We had a sidewalk that was about a third of the way, so I had to make sure they cleared it. They would cross the sidewalk, I would lay it out in front of them, and they would try to make diving catches. It was up to me to make it an amazing catch instead of a routine catch."

Archie's philosophy was simple, but it's not easy for many parents to follow.

"I think you love your kids, just kind of have fun with it, don't get too serious about athletics," he said. "It's got to be fun. If they work at it and become good, it has to be on their own. They've got to want to work at it. Otherwise, just have fun. That's the way it ought to be."

These Manning boys could play just about every sport.

"I think my dad enjoyed us playing sports," Eli said. "He grew up playing sports. A lot of times, with father and son, that brings something in common. One of his favorite things was when we had friends over on the weekends, he loved for us to be outside playing basketball and for him to just coordinate, whether he was the ref or coming up with different games to play if you had an odd number. He encouraged us to be active, and it was all about fun and building some of the character issues that come from playing sports and some of the traits that you learn."

Cooper played some quarterback in high school until he saw an easier path to the field as a wide receiver. He started off as a quarterback in the seventh grade and was the junior varsity quarterback in the ninth grade. When he was a sophomore, he was blocked by a senior starter, and Cooper wanted to play right away. He lobbied to be switched to wide receiver and then lobbied for the system to be changed from a wing-T one-receiver run-dominated formation to two wide receivers.

"I need to be the second one," Cooper told the coaches.

He turned out to be a talented wide receiver, making all-state his junior and senior seasons. His final year, Cooper lit up the Bayou with Peyton as his quarterback.

"Cooper was funny and kind of crazy and he would test you a little bit," Archie said. "Cooper made average grades at Newman. It was hard—but he thought he was the smartest guy in the class."

When Archie and Olivia would attend conferences at Newman with Cooper's teachers and guidance counselors, they received good news and bad news. "Well, Cooper could do a little better," they were told. "He's making Bs and Cs; he could do better."

The good news? "He sure is fun to have," the teachers said.

Peyton competed in the classroom like he did on the football field. He was low-maintenance and in control. "Peyton was kind of straight-ahead, good grades, really worked hard," Archie said. "I'm not sure it was all about gathering all the knowledge he could. He just wanted to be one of the top students. He made good grades. We never had any problems."

Once Eli caught up with his reading, he became an excellent student.

The issue: Could he be as good as Peyton on the football field?

By the time Eli became Newman's starter in his sophomore season, Cooper's football career was over because of the neck injury and Peyton was in his junior season at Tennessee. This was now the third time Archie had been through varsity football at Newman, but his dedication remained the same as the first two times.

"I didn't want Eli to feel the pressure. I don't think he did," Archie said. "Obviously, he wanted to be like Peyton, be good like Peyton, wanted to play college football like Peyton. But he didn't express it. Eli was just quiet. He was happy. I don't know if Eli had as many friends as the others, but if you had Eli as a friend, you had a good friend. Eli just calmly went about his business."

Eli never felt his parents had to worry that he would be disappointed if he didn't equal what his brothers accomplished athletically. He was in it to have fun, and if good things happened as a result, that would make it even better. "I never felt I had to outdo my brothers," Eli said. "I just kind of had my own way of doing things. I was going to work hard. I enjoyed playing quarterback. I enjoyed my friends. I enjoyed playing basketball. I was just trying to win games and enjoy playing high school sports."

One night his senior year he scored 24 points playing basketball and the next night he never took a shot. When the Mannings saw him after each game, Eli had the same expression on his face. "That was just Eli," his father said.

His expressionless face was often confused with indifference or confusion when he struggled in his early years with the Giants. But it was all part of the "Easy" persona. Cooper was such a live wire, and Peyton was so intense, that Eli had to discover how to fit in with their strong personalities. He had some catching up to do to become one of the guys.

"Peyton and I played a lot of sports together," Cooper said. "We fought a lot. A lot of hoops games in the backyard that never finished because the game gets close and here come the elbows and here come the fists. I have very distinct memories of my dad begging and pleading with us, if we could ever get along, how lucky we were to have each other. Just compete and finish a game as opposed to fighting and fighting. You kind of had a built-in friend. We were together a lot, but we battled."

Cooper may not have had great grades, but he was savvy and street-smart. He knew when it was time to get along with Peyton. "When I was a senior in high school, I was a receiver and Peyton was going to be the starting quarterback," he said. "That's when I had to start kissing his butt or he wasn't going to throw it to me."

Newman made it to the semifinals of the state tournament, and Archie and Olivia felt so much pride watching Peyton throw to Cooper. They connected seventy-five times that season.

Cooper's relationship with Eli was of a different nature because of the age difference.

"I was definitely much more of a big brother to Eli," Cooper said. "When I came back from college to New Orleans, I was twenty-two and he was fifteen. That is when we became peers as opposed to the little guy in the background. He was in high school and he was the quarterback. I was working and going to see his games. Peyton wasn't around, and Eli and I got to be more of pals."

By no means was Eli immune from getting tortured by his brothers. Peyton would sit on Eli and bang on his chest until he could name all the schools in the SEC. Peyton could rattle them off in his sleep. Eli didn't care all that much. Once he mastered the names of the SEC schools, Peyton would test him on all the NFL teams. And so it went.

"That's the way it works down the line," Eli said. "The oldest picks on the middle one and the middle one picks on the younger one. You just keep going down a notch. Cooper is seven years older than me; it wasn't even a fair comparison. I don't think he got any enjoyment out of picking on me. It would have been too easy. Every once in a while he wanted to show his power, or I was being annoying like little brothers could be and they picked on me. But nothing terrible. They were both good brothers to me and we had lots of fun and good times."

Eli loved it when Peyton would ask him to catch passes. Peyton was getting bigger and stronger, and his passes had more and more velocity. Not easy for an eleven-year-old to withstand the pounding from the hard throws of a sixteen-year-old high school quarterback with a strong arm.

"The football hurts when somebody is throwing hard," Archie said.

Eli didn't want to disappoint Peyton, so he sold out to make every catch he could. But the constant pounding left him with bruises up and down his chest and arms.

"A lot of times, we'd be throwing in the street. If I dropped it, the ball would get scuffed up," Eli said. "He would get mad at me for not catching it and I'm bruised up."

What to do?

Eli went in the house and found one of his dad's old sweatshirts. He stuffed pillows from the living room couch up and down the sleeves and in front of his chest. Either he would catch Peyton's passes or he could block them with the pillows and the ball would fall gently to the ground without getting scuffed.

"People were looking at us like we were crazy," Eli said. "But it was just kind of what had to get done."

The Manning boys came up with a new nickname for their little brother.

Meet the Michelin Man.

|||||||||||||||||||||||||||||||||||||||||||||||||

Peyton could have gone to any school in the country to play college football. He had more than one hundred schools after him, and by November of his senior year he still had forty on his list. Finally, he narrowed it down to his final four: Tennessee, Florida, Mississippi, and, if he decided to leave the SEC, it was going to be Michigan. If Manning had gone to Michigan for his freshman year in 1994, there's a good chance Michigan would not have recruited Tom Brady, who was one year behind.

Peyton was meticulous as he narrowed down his list. He ultimately ruled out Mississippi, not necessarily because his father was a Rebels legend and he didn't want to deal with the pressure of following in his footsteps but because the school was facing NCAA sanctions and he wanted no part of that.

"Peyton enjoyed recruiting," Archie sad. "He attacked it like he does everything. He had it organized and didn't know where he wanted to go. He did his due diligence."

He would set aside time each night after his schoolwork to speak to coaches. He studied media guides. He became familiar with depth charts and systems. He wanted to know if there was a freshman quarterback on the roster he would have to beat out.

"Peyton's theory was, 'I will commit one week before signing day. So wherever I go, maybe I can help get two or three players to sign that last week.' He had a plan," Archie said.

He chose Tennessee, which turned out to be a great decision. He stayed all four years, despite at one point in his junior year pretty much making up his mind he would declare for the draft. He was on course to graduate in three years. Although Peyton Manning didn't win the Heisman, never beat Florida, and won the SEC only in his senior year, he never regretted picking Tennessee. The state of Mississippi was in an uproar when he didn't choose to go to Archie's school, and some of the folks even blamed Archie, but Archie sat back and let his son make his own decision.

Five years later, it was Eli's turn.

"One thing I learned about parenthood is how different your children are," Archie said.

Eli sat in on many of Peyton's home visits. He would come into the living room and meet the coaches and listen without saying a word. But he was taking it all in. "He was an observer to that whole process," Archie said.

Eli didn't get as much attention as a junior, but there were enough big-time programs after him that he was going to have a difficult decision to make. Tennessee was interested, but he told them early in the process that he had no desire to follow his brother. Pressure rarely gets to Eli, but this would have been unbearable. Every step of the way, he would have been compared to his big brother. It was difficult enough at Newman, but that school felt like home to Eli, and high school expectations don't come close to college expectations.

He didn't want to turn his recruiting into a long process. He told Archie he had no plans to visit more than a handful of schools. Fewer than five. He narrowed his list quickly. He immediately eliminated Tennessee when they began recruiting him.

He didn't lead them on when they first made contact. "The first thing Eli said was, 'I'm not coming to Tennessee. Don't even recruit me,'" Archie said.

Eli had been in Peyton's shadow from the moment he stepped on the field at Newman. It was different from the pressure Peyton felt trying to live up to the Manning name. The time lapse between Archie's last year in the NFL to Peyton playing college ball was ten years. By that time, Archie said, "there was a generation that didn't remember I had played."

Eli was just five years behind Peyton, and he was following the same path. "When he played in high school, he played at Newman and everybody remembered what Peyton did," Archie said. "He was playing college ball in the SEC and it was still fresh what Peyton did. He was under more pressure. I can't say he felt it, but still it was there."

He visited Texas during his senior year. He went to Virginia immediately after the season was over. He had visited Ole Miss his entire life. His intention was to commit one week after the season ended.

"He didn't want to wait," Archie said. "He didn't want to go through it."

It came down to Texas and Ole Miss. Archie was convinced that Eli didn't want to go to Ole Miss. But then Mississippi coach Tommy Tuberville was hired as the head coach at Auburn after the 1998 season. Mississippi then hired David Cutcliffe, who had been Peyton's offensive coordinator and quarterbacks coach at Tennessee. Eli told Archie he wanted to go to Ole Miss for a visit.

"He said, 'I want to go tomorrow,'" Archie said.

Cutcliffe wanted Eli, who made the visit to Oxford, Mississippi, returned to New Orleans, and committed the next day. "All along he wanted to go to Ole Miss. That's where he wanted to go to college," Archie said. "I was just not sure where he wanted to play football. He didn't want to go to Tennessee. When Cut went to Mississippi, that was a double dip. It was the school he wanted to go to and the coach he wanted to play for."

Cutcliffe and Peyton "were as close as any player-coach I've ever seen," Archie said. "Still are."

When Cutcliffe was fired by Ole Miss after the 2004 season, he worked as an assistant for one year at Notre Dame, and two years back at Tennessee, before Duke hired him as head coach in 2008. He remains very tight with the Manning family. He supervised Peyton's workouts at Duke when he was making a comeback in 2012 after missing the previous season following his fourth neck surgery. After Peyton signed with Denver, he would bring his Broncos receivers to Durham, North Carolina, for off-season workouts at Duke. Eli would also bring in his Giants receivers.

When Eli showed up at Oxford to begin his college career, the last thing he was feeling was pressure to duplicate his father's achievements. "God, that had to be over thirty years ago," Archie said.

Peyton could recite every one of Archie's stats, name his teammates, list all the honors on his résumé. Eli was either disinterested or oblivious.

"Eli had heard a lot about me; he had heard how great I was at Ole Miss, but he never dug in, never paid much attention to it," Archie said.

He just wasn't intimidated by having to live up to his father's legacy. "It was just a long gap in between," Eli said. "It wouldn't be like any of the teammates I was playing with would have remembered my dad. They might know the name, [but] they wouldn't remember him playing. I don't remember him playing football. I didn't see it as being a big deal. I think Ole Miss was the right spot for me. It was where I wanted to go. It just seemed like a great fit with Coach Cutcliffe and the staff they had. It made the most sense for me."

One day, Eli decided to look at the Ole Miss media guide. He was anticipating seeing big numbers next to his father's name. But back in the day when Archie played college football, it was not the wide-open passing game it was when Eli played. "If I threw for 180 yards, that was a big game," Archie said. "I had a couple of big games with 400 yards and 300 yards."

Eli couldn't believe what he was seeing in the media guide. "He did run for a lot of yards, but he threw more interceptions than touchdowns. Not many touchdowns." He laughed. "So I had to bring him back down," Eli said.

Archie passed along the genes for a strong arm to his sons. He kept the running genes for himself. He was as dangerous running the ball as throwing it. He would often run fifteen times per game. Peyton and Eli were not gifted with speed or the desire to venture far from the pocket.

On the day Eli was looking through his father's records in the Ole Miss media guide when he was on campus, he was so unimpressed, he called home.

"You know, Dad, your numbers weren't very good," Eli said.

"They really weren't," Archie said.

On the Ole Miss campus, there is a "Speed Limit 18" sign. That's for Archie, who wore number 18. Now there is a "Speed Limit 10" sign. That's for Eli, who wore number 10.

If Peyton had decided to attend Mississippi, he would have known of his father's accomplishments far in advance of his first practice. Archie loved that about him. "Peyton was always so interested," Archie said. "Cooper loved sports and knew sports. But Peyton was interested in sports, he was interested in my career, more so than the other two."

Peyton learned about his father's college teammates from the radio tapes of games Ole Miss had sent Archie. He would sit there and listen to Stan Torgerson call the games, with Lyman Hellums providing the analysis. "Peyton was ten or twelve years old and he would listen to those games," Archie said. "So he knew the players. He knew my teammates. He asked a lot of questions. We were blessed with all of our children. Peyton was the easy one to raise. He did his schoolwork. He did what he was told. He really tried to please his parents, his teachers, and people."

||||||||||||||||||||||||||||||||||||||||||||||

Giants general manager Ernie Accorsi fell in love with Eli Manning during his junior year at Ole Miss. He wrote up a glowing scouting report and advised his scouting staff that he would do all he could to get him if he left school early and declared for the 2003 draft. Manning remained in school for his senior year, and Accorsi kept an eye on him, but he didn't revise much in his scouting report one year later.

The Giants went through an injury-ravaged season in 2003, finished 4-12, and Coach Jim Fassel was fired. Kerry Collins, a veteran who had taken the Giants to the Super Bowl in 2000 but then proceeded to throw four interceptions in the loss to the Ravens, was the incumbent quarterback. If Manning had come out the previous year, it was unlikely the Giants could have gotten him. They were picking twenty-fifth after making the play-offs in 2002.

But the 2004 draft provided them with an opportunity to get their quarterback of the future. Collins had peaked in 2000, and Accorsi was a believer that a team could not win the Super Bowl without a franchise quarterback. He was with Johnny Unitas in Baltimore, and he drafted John Elway for the Colts before owner Robert Irsay traded him away one week after

Accorsi selected him. Elway didn't want to play for Irsay, and Irsay didn't want to pay him anyway.

Accorsi was enamored of Eli Manning. He was not as good a prospect as Peyton, but he had the good bloodline; and in a strong quarterback year, that's who Accorsi wanted. His backup plan was Ben Roethlisberger from Miami of Ohio. Philip Rivers from North Carolina State was the other elite quarterback available, but Accorsi was not interested.

Accorsi began to have trade discussions with Chargers general manager A. J. Smith. San Diego had the first pick and the Giants had the fourth pick. San Diego liked Rivers best, after Marty Schottenheimer and the Chargers' coaching staff had worked with him in the Senior Bowl in Mobile, Alabama. Manning had the most value. Smith told the Giants GM he was willing to do a deal, but the price was very steep. In addition to high draft picks, Smith also wanted pass rusher Osi Umenyiora, who was the Giants' second-round pick in 2003. Accorsi valued pass rushers just below quarterbacks on his list of must-have players.

Accorsi and Smith were playing a game of chicken. Accorsi knew Smith wanted Rivers but didn't want to pick him first when he was not projected to go that high. Smith knew Accorsi wanted Manning but he was not going to let Manning get that far. Eli was an asset and Smith wanted to be compensated.

Just three days before the draft, word got out that Tom Condon, Manning's agent, at Archie's direction, had confirmed to Smith that Eli would not play for the Chargers. It was similar to what Elway did in 1983. It was not a secret within the league that Manning wanted no part of the Chargers, who were considered dysfunctional. NFL commissioner Paul Tagliabue had taken the unusual step of getting involved when he called Archie and asked him to meet with Chargers president Dean Spanos. They met in Mississippi. Spanos asked Archie if he would speak with Schottenheimer.

San Diego was not a highly regarded organization and always had trouble getting top picks signed; Manning wanted to play for the Giants. Interestingly, six years earlier, the Colts had the first overall pick and the Chargers had the second pick. Until the night before the draft, the Colts had kept a secret of whether they intended to take Peyton Manning or Ryan Leaf. Peyton had voiced no objection to being drafted by the Chargers.

Archie was accused of steering Eli away from the Chargers because he didn't want his son to go through the tough times he experienced in New Orleans. Archie accepted the Chargers' invitation to meet with team officials in San Diego the Tuesday before the draft. He had dinner with Smith, Schottenheimer, and Spanos, and they tried to convince him that San Diego was the right spot for Eli. Adding to the intrigue, Accorsi's best friend in football was Schottenheimer.

It was drama at draft time. Was Archie being overbearing?

"We had Archie Manning in here for a visit," Smith said back then. "He met the staff and things of that nature. We went out to dinner with him. Obviously his son Eli is a consideration for us. When we did our quarterback tour, Archie did not attend. Archie is more than just a father with his boys. He's a football guy."

The next day, Condon called Smith and told him not to take Eli.

"I've got to huddle with Eli and Tom and see where we are on this thing," Archie said. "The only thing I'll say is I never talked to the Chargers about the Giants. I was asked to come to San Diego and see them."

The Mannings were already in New York for the draft when the story broke. The next day, Archie, Peyton, and Eli were at an event at Tavern on the Green in Central Park that had been set up long before Eli's destination became a controversy. The Mannings announced that Eli didn't want to play for the Chargers.

"This was done with reluctance," Archie said. "I'm sorry about that. But that's the way it is."

"It's the right thing to do," Peyton said.

"It's not the way we planned things. That's the way it goes," Eli said.

There was tension at the Theater at Madison Square Garden on draft day. The Mannings were being severely criticized for attempting to manipulate the draft. How dare a college kid tell the NFL where he does and doesn't want to play?

Accorsi and Smith continued to talk but could not come to an agreement on a trade. They didn't even speak the day before the draft or the morning of the draft before it started at noon. Accorsi was not worried. He had been tipped off by a source he trusted that Smith would take Manning at number 1, and then when the Giants were on the clock at number 4, he would call Accorsi. Who would blink first? The Chargers didn't even want Manning. They wanted Rivers. Accorsi knew not to call Smith before the draft. He knew he would lose his leverage. He knew Smith didn't want Manning and would come back to him.

There was risk involved. What happened if the Raiders, picking second, or the Cardinals, picking third, decided to take Rivers? Then the Chargers would be stuck with a player who didn't want to play for them. What happened if either the Raiders or the Cardinals decided to trade their pick to a team that wanted Rivers?

The pieces fell neatly into place after the Chargers selected Manning. The Raiders picked Iowa offensive tackle Robert Gallery, and the Cardinals picked Pittsburgh receiver Larry Fitzgerald. Then, just as Accorsi was tipped off would happen, Smith called him with seven and a half minutes remaining of the fifteen minutes the Giants were allotted to make their choice. Accorsi knew all along he was dealing from a position of strength. If he couldn't get Manning, he would be more than happy to take Big Ben Roethlisberger. Smith again asked for Umenyiora.

Accorsi told him again he was untouchable. They finally settled on an exchange of draft picks and the Giants' selecting Rivers for the Chargers. Accorsi confirmed with Smith that it was Rivers whom San Diego wanted. Once the Giants selected Rivers, the trade was called in to the league office. Rules prohibited the Chargers from simply trading Manning's rights to the Giants. The Giants first had to make a selection. Accorsi trusted Smith, even though he didn't know him very well, not to back out of the deal once the Giants took Rivers.

Manning first walked onto the stage at the Theater holding a Chargers cap. He was booed by the fans who felt he was being a spoiled brat. Less than an hour later, he was holding a Giants cap after being informed by a kid in a back hallway that the trade had gone through and his new football home was just fifteen minutes away on the other side of the Hudson River.

Archie had run interference for Eli and let the responsibility and criticism fall on him. Eli never felt the anti-Archie talk was fair. He appreciated his father standing up for him but said the decision was his.

Years later, Eli set the record straight. He had just finished a minicamp practice led by Giants then-rookie coach Ben McAdoo. He was seated on a couch just inside the back door of the team facility around the corner from the Vince Lombardi trophies he helped the Giants win in Super Bowls XLII and XLVI with victories against the New England Patriots.

"It was never my father's decision. It wasn't him getting involved telling me what to do," Eli said. "It had nothing to do with that. When I told him I knew what my plan was, he said, 'You're going to take some heat for this.' I said, 'I know.' He was just the spokesman for me, so I wasn't right in the center of it having to answer all the questions and taking all the heat. He said he would handle some of that and try to explain it and take some attention away from me. He was doing me a favor, and it made it look like he was the one making the decision."

John Elway, who at the time was general manager of the Colorado Crush in the Arena Football League, watched the Manning situation unfold. It was not unlike the power play he'd pulled on the Colts in 1983 that ended with his being traded to the Broncos one week after the draft.

"I support Eli one hundred percent," he said. "I'm happy this worked out for him. Now his work has begun. You come out of college with high expectations. Now he's got to go out and prove himself."

Manning was just two years old when Elway imposed his will on the draft. Manning followed the script to perfection. He threatened to go back to school for one more year and reenter the draft. Elway threatened to play baseball for one year and reenter the draft. They each got their way.

"I've heard it talked about over the years," Eli said. "I don't know the whole situation of what [Elway] went through or his reasoning. I don't know if it compares to my situation."

Archie Manning was by his son's side to attempt to shield him from the criticism just as Jack Elway, John's father, was the messenger telling the Colts not to pick his son John in 1983.

Crybaby? Spoiled brat?

"It is hard to go through," Elway said. "The hardest thing is the impression it's so taboo for a player to try and go someplace where you'd like to go. You are perceived as, 'Who is this kid to try and manipulate the draft and dictate where he wants to go?' That part still amazes me. It takes time to go away. Why is there the perception of being a spoiled brat? If you've got some talent and you're in demand, why not try to go someplace where you can be happy? I totally understand Archie trying to get him to New York."

Eli's career got off to a rough start. After he was inserted as the starter by Tom Coughlin, replacing Kurt Warner in the tenth game of the season, when the Giants were 5-4, he lost his first six starts before a comeback victory against the Cowboys in the final game. The Giants made the play-offs in Manning's first two full seasons as the starter in 2005 and 2006 but did not win a play-off game.

Was Eli the right man for the job? Did Accorsi make a mistake? His play was wildly inconsistent.

Manning led the Giants to the play-offs in 2007 for the third consecutive season. They finished with a 10-6 record in the regular season and were seeded fifth in the NFC. They had gone all-out against the undefeated Patriots in the final game before the play-offs to try to gain some momentum. They played New England tough and had the lead in the third quarter before Tom Brady rallied the Patriots to a 38–35 victory.

New York then went into Tampa, Dallas, and Green Bay and won in consecutive weeks in the postseason to advance to the Super Bowl, where the Giants were fourteen-point underdogs against the Patriots at University of Phoenix Stadium in Glendale, Arizona. Despite the long-shot odds, the Giants had a lot of confidence, knowing they nearly beat New England just five weeks earlier.

The Giants trailed 14–10 after Brady connected with Randy Moss on a 6-yard touchdown pass with just under three minutes remaining.

Archie and his wife, Olivia, were sitting in a suite provided by NBC. Peyton was invited to sit with them.

"You sit with us," Archie said to Peyton.

"I'll be all right," Peyton said.

Peyton was sitting in the Gatorade suite. He knew the

cameras always found Archie at his sons' games, and Peyton didn't want any part of that. He stood in a corner of the suite and watched the game by himself. "I kind of assumed he was going to sit with us," Archie said. "He never even considered it."

Now Eli had the ball down by three with a bunch of nervous Mannings in the house as the little brother tried to end the Patriots' quest to be the first 19-0 team in NFL history. The now historic 32-yard "Helmet Catch" by David Tyree, after Manning had wiggled his way out of the grasp of several Patriots defenders, set up Manning's 13-yard game-winning touchdown pass to Plaxico Burress with 39 seconds left in the game.

No surprise, but the cameras found Peyton. He was smiling and clapping. It was a nice scene in the locker room after the game with Peyton standing next to Eli as they dissected the final drive together.

"Peyton has always taken great pride in Eli," Archie said. "He was a great mentor to Eli and always went out of his way to mentor him. The funniest thing is when Eli got into the league, everybody assumed this was going to be some great rivalry. They would go at each other at the kitchen table, but they hated playing against each other."

Eli's refusal to play for the Chargers worked out just fine. Just as Elway's threats against the Colts let him escape what he felt was going to be a bad situation.

Elway played in five Super Bowls for Denver and won the last two. Manning played in two Super Bowls in his first thirteen seasons, won them both, and was named Super Bowl MVP each time. It worked out just as planned for Elway and

Manning. The Colts came out on the short side of the Elway trade and didn't get back to the Super Bowl until Eli's brother Peyton took them. Rivers didn't make it to the Super Bowl in his first thirteen years with the Chargers.

Between Eli and Peyton, they have won four Super Bowls and three Super Bowl MVPs.

"I've got to pinch myself," Archie said. "I don't have a 'love me' room in my house. I have one in my office."

On a shelf in his office are four 8-by-10 photos, two with Peyton, two with Eli, showing them holding the Lombardi Trophy. That's why the Mannings are considered the First Family of Football.

"Four times," Archie said. "That's pretty cool."

JAMEIS WINSTON

Jaboo and Ant

Jaboo Winston was only four years old when his father, Antonor, dressed him in a football uniform and allowed him to practice and play in games with seven- and eight-year-old boys.

"He was forty-two or forty-four pounds and played tight end and defensive tackle," he said. "He started every game at four years old."

Jaboo soon became a child prodigy with a football in his hands. He could sling it. At age seven, he was throwing the ball 45 yards. "He threw a natural, beautiful ball," his dad said.

By the time he got to Florida State, he was one of the most accomplished two-sport stars in the country out of Hueytown High School in Alabama, highly recruited as a quarterback in football and a pitcher/outfielder in baseball. He was drafted by the Texas Rangers in the fifteenth round in his senior year at Hueytown, but he wanted to play football and baseball in college. He won the Heisman Trophy as a redshirt freshman at Florida State in 2013, and at the time he was the youngest player ever to win it at 19 years, 342 days. Louisville quarterback Lamar Jackson was four days younger when he won it three years later. Now Winston is one of the youngest quarterbacks in the NFL after the Tampa Bay Buccaneers made him the first overall pick of the 2015 draft.

Antonor Winston has been with him every step of the way.

"My dad doesn't want to take credit for baseball, but for every sport I was introduced to, he was the main one teaching me everything I know," Winston said. "He taught me how to throw a football. He taught me how to swing a baseball bat. Even though it wasn't pretty, he still taught me. He went out of his way to make sure I was a great student, and he wanted to make sure I was one of the best kids in all of youth sports."

The first thing that becomes clear about Antonor Winston is that he can be very difficult to understand. His accent is Alabama-thick. He is from the Deep South and sounds like it. "I have trouble understanding my dad," Winston said, laughing.

The second thing is that he rarely calls his son by his given name, Jameis. His wife nicknamed him "Little-J-boo" when he was born on January 6, 1994. That soon became "Boo," until it became "Jaboo." Anybody in his inner circle or anyone who has known him from his childhood in Alabama calls him Jaboo. Jameis is his football stage name. Just like how Tom Brady is never called "Tommy" in the media or by Patriots fans, but his parents, his wife, his sisters, and his closest friends all call him Tommy.

Shortening names seems to be a Winston thing. Antonor goes by Ant.

Winston won the starting job in Tampa in training camp over returning veteran Mike Glennon and has started since the first game of his rookie year. The very first pass he threw in a regular season game in the Bucs season opener was intercepted and returned for a touchdown by the Tennessee Titans. The last quarterback to get off to such an inauspicious start was Brett Favre with the Atlanta Falcons in 1991. Favre was traded after his rookie season and went on to have a Hall of Fame career with the Green Bay Packers. The Bucs plan to hang on to Winston for a long time.

Antonor Winston put a football in Jameis's hands early. Though he wasn't his first football coach when Jaboo was playing on a team at the age of four, he coached him after that until he got to middle school. It wasn't easy for Ant. He worked for the city road maintenance department in Bessemer, Alabama, home of Bo Jackson, population 27,000. He would report at three in the morning and work until three in the afternoon. Antonor worked on the highway crews that painted the lines in the road and repaired the broken stoplights in town. "When you are driving at night and see the workers on the road, and the roads are blocked off, that's what he did," Jameis said.

Ant was coaching youth football in Bessemer, which is southwest of Birmingham. Even when Jameis was too young to play, Ant still was coaching. Jameis was only two or three when he began accompanying his father to practice. He would throw the ball around and then started putting on shoulder pads and helmets to see how they felt. He soon was playing with kids three and four years older than him in an under-seventy-five-pound league.

"I actually played true tackle football with kids who were older than me," he said. "When I was seven, my age-group caught up with me. That's when stuff got a little easier."

Ant became his football coach when Jameis was six years old, and that was the arrangement until he was twelve. "I stepped right in then," he said. "I'm not saying we didn't think Jameis would be a football player, but I didn't think he would be a Heisman Trophy winner."

Ant loves football and knew a lot about it. But he didn't show any favoritism to Jameis. "One of my good friends, Jevon Long, we had basically known each other since we came out of the womb," Jameis said. "That was my dad's favorite player. Every coach has his favorite and I'm thinking, because I'm his son, I should be the favorite. He was not only hard on me, but he would go overboard when I did something wrong. I could score a touchdown, but if I did it the wrong way, he would yell at me. It was not in a way to embarrass me in front of the other parents, but he always held me to a higher standard."

It became a little easier the second year he played for his father. He was now seven years old and playing against kids his own age. He knew his father would continue to be tough on him, but Jameis never once asked him to let up or have some-body else coach him. Sports is supposed to be all about having fun at that age. High school is too far away. Minds and bodies are developing. But Antonor already wanted Jameis to learn life lessons through sports.

"My dad always taught me life isn't easy," he said. "He always used to tell me he didn't grow up with a dad. He used to say, 'Don't let your excuses get in the way of your dreams.' There's actually a lot of people who didn't have father figures, but they had different people in their lives who affected them in a positive way."

Winston went to live in nearby Hueytown for a few years with his grandmother. That was part of the way of life for the Winston family. It was a full house. "I had a huge family," he said. "The majority of my family lived in my grandmother's house."

The Winstons soon all moved from Bessemer. Ant and his wife, Loretta, bought a house in Hueytown when Jameis was eight. He became a star at Hueytown High School in baseball and football, but there was racial tension. "I was the first African American quarterback at that high school," he said. "It was difficult, but one thing my dad always taught me is sports bring people closer together. I truly believe that."

Winston feels the folks in Hueytown were searching for the next great white hope and he was not it. "They weren't looking for a black kid to come in there and be productive and be active and make straight As in school and also excel in sports," he said. "I just had to be twice as good as everyone."

Quarterbacks are leaders. They must bring everybody in the huddle together. Baseball is different. It's a team game, but more of an individual sport. Many of the white kids Winston became friends with were on the high school baseball team. "I probably faced more prejudices in baseball than football," he said.

When he was in the second grade, he was suspended for punching a kid in the lunchroom. Winston said he was retaliating.

"They didn't get suspended, but somehow I got suspended," he said. "There was just a lot of different situations I had to deal with back then."

He didn't express frustration to his father about any prejudice he might have been feeling or facing. "I came home and I was consumed with sports," he said. "Sports helped me get away from the reality I was living in. I loved my teammates. White, black, Mexican, green—I got to fight with those people on the field. I got to compete with them every day. That's what my dad taught me. My dad taught me to love everyone; and we can't let other people's emotions, other people's feelings, distract me from my goal."

Trouble would follow Winston when he arrived at Florida State. But first, he had to get there.

||||||||||||||||||||||||||||||||||||||||||||||

Jameis Winston was becoming a big name in high school sports in Alabama. He started getting recruited by major colleges for football in the ninth grade. That can be overwhelming for a teenager, especially for a kid barely in his teens. Winston embraced the process.

"It was just my dream," he said. "My dad did a good job of preparing me for it. I feel like I am a strong-willed individual. My dad always told me to live by three things: God, school, and anything you put your mind to. I definitely put my mind to that. I was going to get a scholarship. One thing he told me is, 'Hey, man, you want to go to college for free. I don't have enough money to be paying for no college,' and I knew he didn't, so I was motivated by that."

He was on the proper stage. Hueytown had an excellent football program. Winston was quickly finding out he was going to have some choices, some really good choices, of where he wanted to go to college. "Football in Alabama is the biggest thing in our state," he said. "We don't have any pro teams to take our mind off football. We have Alabama and we have Auburn. It doesn't matter if it's a low A team or it's the highest A team where they have three thousand kids in their high school, you're going to have at least sixty kids on each football team in Alabama no matter what classification you are in."

Four high schools in the area really went at it. Bessemer City was where Winston's mother went to school. His father went to Hueytown. McAdory was where local legend Bo Jackson went a few decades earlier. And there was Pleasant Grove. "All four of those schools were in a three-mile radius," Winston said. "Our biggest rivalry was with Pleasant Grove."

Now that Winston was being coached in high school, his father was not in the position to be quite as hands-on. But he still stayed on his son about things he needed to keep improving. "I wasn't getting much praise when I came home," he said. "It was always some kind of critiquing or coaching. It was never a pat on the back besides bringing home straight As. If it's a football game, I did something wrong. That's what helped me get that perfectionist mentality. My dad is a coach. Everyone calls my dad Coach Ant. Even his close friends call him Coach Ant."

Alabama coach Nick Saban visited Winston's house to make his pitch. So did Florida State's Jimbo Fisher. Winston really liked Stanford and LSU. Even though Bo Jackson played baseball and football at Auburn, and Winston wanted to play both in college, Auburn was not a consideration. Auburn committed a violation when an assistant coach had impermissible contact with Winston during an event called "Tiger Prowl." Auburn briefly disciplined two assistant coaches but the school was not allowed to have any on-campus contact with Winston until January of his senior year in 2012, although he visited in March 2011.

"When I was in the tenth grade, I actually got put on probation with Auburn for some type of illegal recruiting technique that they tried to use," Winston said. "They had actually come to my school. Auburn used to do something with this big RV. They used to have limos drive around the state of Alabama to the schools of their highest recruits and just basically show up."

Auburn did not commit a violation by allowing Winston on the recruiting bus, but the contact with the assistant coach caused a problem. Although Auburn ultimately offered him a scholarship, they were off his list. Texas was the school that most interested Winston, but they didn't offer him. They didn't even return his phone calls.

Alabama was intriguing. It's not easy to turn down Saban after he sits in your living room. A. J. McCarron was the Crimson Tide quarterback and would have two years of eligibility remaining when Winston arrived if he chose Alabama. He was a good enough college player that Winston might have been forced to sit on the bench. But Winston was talented enough that he might have beaten out McCarron. That was not an issue. The Seminoles were set at quarterback, too, with senior E. J. Manuel in 2012. He was later drafted in the first round by the Buffalo Bills after a 25-6 record starting at Florida State.

Matt Scott, who was the Hueytown football coach when Winston attended, had been put in charge of recruiting by Antonor. He became the point man. How could Winston not go to Alabama?

"What happened is, the truth of that story is not sexy enough for everybody," Scott told AL.com. "Everybody wants to say he didn't go to Alabama because they didn't let him play baseball. That's ridiculous. That's 100 percent false. Coach Saban said he could play baseball. We had a plan mapped out on how he would do that.

"Or they say Alabama is not going to play a black quarterback. We both laughed about that. Jameis and I knew Coach Saban well enough to know that he's so competitive that there's no way he's going to make a decision based on the color of his skin. Nothing is going to influence him to do that. In our mind, that was ridiculous. Alabama did a great job recruiting Jameis."

Winston wanted a new environment. He wanted to get out of Alabama, and Tuscaloosa was too close. "Alabama was thirty-five minutes away from my house," he said. "At least Auburn was two hours away. I liked Auburn because they had just had Cam Newton. Why aren't you recruiting me? I found out the reason why they weren't recruiting me when it was too late."

Winston was subjected to a lot of pressure to choose Alabama or Auburn. High school football stars in Alabama are expected to remain in-state to play college ball. Winston committed to Florida State one month before his senior year at Hueytown. "That's where I got the most racism that I actually experienced with trying to leave that state," he said. "My grandmother received hate voice messages at work. She worked at a hospital. I guess people knew how to get in contact with her. In Hueytown, you are either Auburn or Alabama. My parents went through a lot. They were the ones that had to sit in the stands while I was out there playing. They were the ones trying to protect me from everything that was happening around them, but they couldn't because it was obvious. It is what it is."

Baseball turned out to be the deciding factor when Winston chose Florida State. He didn't believe Alabama or Auburn had a good enough baseball program. He wanted to go to a school that had a history of players who played two sports. Jackson was a Heisman winner at Auburn who also excelled at baseball, but the recruiting issues eliminated Auburn. He developed a close relationship with Saban. His parents wanted him to go to Stanford, but Winston said it was too far from home.

"I chose Florida State because it felt so Alabama to me," he said. "It felt like Tallahassee wasn't the Florida I was expecting. I was expecting eighty degrees every day, a cool breeze, have a good time. I wasn't expecting Tallahassee to be exactly like Alabama. It caught me off guard. Tampa is more like the Florida I expected."

Winston was redshirted his freshman year at Florida State as Manuel finished his college career. He took over his second year and the Seminoles won the national championship, beating

Auburn, of all teams, 34–31, to complete a perfect 14-0 season in the final year before the NCAA went to a four-team play-off system. Winston was named the game's most valuable offensive player after completing 20 of 35 passes for 237 yards and two touchdowns. He brought the Seminoles back from a 21–3 deficit in the second quarter—the largest comeback in a Bowl Championship Series game. Winston drove the Seminoles 80 yards for the winning score after they fell behind 31–27 with 1:19 remaining. His 2-yard touchdown pass to Kelvin Benjamin with 13 seconds left won the game.

Winston had Florida State back in the play-offs the next year in what turned out to be his final season. They were torched by Oregon 59–20 in the semifinal game. Winston had impressive but misleading stats: He completed 29 of 45 passes for 348 yards with one touchdown and one interception. But with his team trailing 39–20 in the third quarter, he dropped the ball after slipping in the backfield and Oregon returned it 58 yards for a touchdown. The loss ended the Seminoles' twenty-nine-game winning streak.

By then it was clear that Winston had played his final game for Florida State. A series of off-the-field transgressions made it impossible for him to return. During a two-year period starting on December 8, 2012, when he was accused of raping a woman at his off-campus apartment, he was involved in so many issues that it became imperative for him to get out of Tallahassee and get a fresh start. His reputation and his future were in jeopardy.

He was never charged in the rape case. He was accused of taking a woman from a bar to his apartment and sexually assaulting her. She claimed she was drunk. He said the sex was consensual. She sued him in April 2015 for sexual battery, assault, false imprisonment, and emotional distress. The woman filed the lawsuit two weeks before the Bucs drafted Winston in 2015. The woman settled a Title IX lawsuit against Florida State for $950,000. Winston and the woman settled the civil lawsuit she brought against him in December 2016.

Antonor Winston never stopped believing in his son. If Jameis ever needed his father to stand beside him and support him, this was the time. "He was raised in a positive manner," Antonor said. "We have the closest father-son relationship you can have. The only way he would have to lean on my shoulder or be insecure was if he did it. We are positive people. This could have been racism. He never was charged. We are Hueytown strong."

He also told the *Miami Herald*, "How did I know my son was innocent? Because I raised him. It's simple. The same way y'all should have known he was innocent when he never got picked up or never got charged."

In July 2013, Winston was accused of taking a cup of water at a Burger King, dumping it out, and refilling it several times with soda from a fountain machine. Charges were not filed. He was accused nine months later of stealing $32.72 in crab legs from a Tallahassee supermarket. He claimed he forgot to pay and apologized. In September 2014, Fisher suspended Winston for the first half of the next game on the schedule, which was against Clemson, after Winston jumped onto a table near the FSU student union and screamed a sexually charged obscenity.

After that incident, Winston issued a statement: "First of all,

I want to apologize to the university, my coaches, and to my teammates. I'm not a 'me' person, but in that situation, it was a selfish act, and that's not how you do things around here."

When Winston was drafted by the Texas Rangers out of high school, his father wouldn't let him sign. "We were not a rich family. We were a low-income family," Antonor said. "Why do you think he didn't go?"

He paused for a minute, then provided his own answer. "He wasn't mature," he said. "I wasn't going to put Jaboo on a bus and he would be traveling with some players who got dropped down, some trying to make it up. What I told him was, 'You go to college, man. I don't care how much they offer. Go to college, get mature, go get your degree.'"

His father was right. Jameis wasn't mature enough even when he was surrounded by kids his own age in what should have been a structured, controlled environment with the FSU football team. The world might have swallowed him up if he was riding late-night buses around Texas or the Southwest with players three and four years older than him. It was fine to be around older kids when he was four years old and his father was there to protect him if it got too rough playing with seven-year-olds. Nobody would be there to protect him in the minor leagues. He got into enough trouble at Florida State when he was old enough to know much better.

Winston needed his father to have his back. He was facing serious accusations.

"He didn't get charged with sexual assault or rape," Antonor said.

"My dad knows who I am," Winston said. "As soon as they vindicated me, cleared me of any of those false accusations, we were good. We were not going to associate ourselves or spend time having conversations about things like that. After that, we spent more quality time and had conversations about how to stay away from situations like that."

His father's goal for Jameis at Florida State was for him to mature and get his degree. "Our goal wasn't to go to school for two years," Antonor said.

Jameis left before he would get his degree. Antonor felt that the adversity Jaboo faced at Florida State forced him to grow up and mature. "If you can't get ready after that, you're probably not going to be ready," he said.

It was Jameis's decision to leave school early. It came with his father's blessing.

Winston was fully vetted by the Bucs before they made him the first pick in 2015. They had a choice of Winston or Oregon's Marcus Mariota, who had no personal red flags on his résumé. From a marketing standpoint, Mariota was the safer choice, a clean-cut kid from the University of Oregon who had grown up out of the spotlight in Hawaii. But his game did not translate as well to the NFL as Winston's, even though he outplayed him in the college play-off game. He worked out of the shotgun at Oregon, and players like Robert Griffin III and Johnny Manziel and Tim Tebow failed miserably trying to transition to a regular pro-style offense. Winston could run the ball, but his game was more that of a straight drop-back passer.

The consensus in Tampa was that Winston had a bigger

upside and a better chance to adapt to the NFL passing game. The downside was his history of making bad decisions and finding trouble. The Bucs were going to be making a fully guaranteed investment of $25.3 million over four years to whomever they picked, so they could not afford to make a mistake. Teams that draft a quarterback in the top 10 who ends up a bust— Ryan Leaf and Jamarcus Russell, for examples—are set back five years in their development.

The Bucs had to be sure they could count on Winston. He felt secure that he could count on his father for guidance. "His basic lessons that he taught me when I was growing up go back to when he was my coach in Little League football," Winston said. "How he treated me compared to how he treated everyone else prepared me for the microscope that people put me under, prepared me for this 'celebrity' life now. Everyone is going to view me and look at me and judge me harder than they view other people. Not just because of who I am but frankly because of my position. The way he helped me mentally, showing me since day one you have to be twice as good as anybody else. You can't give anyone a reason to say anything about you."

That all sounds good. Now it will be Winston's job to live up to it.

He quickly became a role model and a leader in the Tampa community after he was drafted. He has not run into any legal issues off the field. He has matured, but that is not to say he is all grown up. Two months into the Bucs' off-season following his second year, Winston volunteered to speak to third-, fourth-, and fifth-grade students at Melrose Elementary School in St. Petersburg. He was trying to convey the message that the world presents many opportunities and it was up to the students to take advantage of them.

He repeated the three rules his father had set out for him when he was their age: God, school, and anything he set his mind to.

One of the boys wasn't paying attention, and Winston wanted to teach him a life lesson as his father had done. He had good intentions, but his message went off the tracks: "All my young boys, stand up. The ladies, sit down. But all my boys, stand up. We strong, right? We strong! We strong, right? All my boys, tell me one time: I can do anything I put my mind to. Now a lot of boys aren't supposed to be soft-spoken. You know what I'm saying. One day y'all are going to have a very deep voice like this. One day, you'll have a very, very deep voice."

Winston should have stopped right there. He didn't.

"But the ladies, they're supposed to be silent, polite, gentle. My men, my men [are] supposed to be strong. I want y'all to tell me what the third rule of life is: I can do anything I put my mind to. Scream it!"

The pushback was immediate. The talk was taped and immediately went viral. One of the girls told her teacher, "I'm strong, too."

Winston's chat was interpreted as being disrespectful to girls and women. The fallout: His thinking was backward. Women were indeed strong. The message he sent in the classroom that day was a bad one, especially for a man who had once been accused of, if not charged with, raping a woman. He needed to be extra careful in his talk to young boys and girls and he was not.

He was trying to do good, and it ended with his issuing an apology.

"I was making an effort to interact with a young male in the audience who didn't seem to be paying attention, and I didn't want to single him out so I asked all the boys to stand up," Winston said. "During my talk, I used a poor word choice that may have overshadowed that positive message for some."

|||||||||||||||||||||||||||||||||||||||||||||||

Jameis won the Heisman Trophy, he was the quarterback of an undefeated team at Florida State that won the national championship, and he's developing into an excellent NFL quarterback. He can only imagine the look on Ant's face if he were to lead the Bucs to the Super Bowl and stand on the podium in the middle of the field holding up the Vince Lombardi Trophy with confetti floating on top of him.

"I think that would be a happy day in everyone's life," Winston said.

Actually, the first thing the son would have to do is make sure the father is at the game.

Antonor Winston is not fond of flying. When Florida State played Auburn for the national championship, the game was in the Rose Bowl in Pasadena, California. Antonor was not sure he could be on a plane that long.

"You got to go, Dad. It's the national championship. You got to go," Jameis said.

"Man, I hate airplanes," Antonor said.

He made the trip. "I guess it messes with his stomach," Jameis said. "Ever since then, he's been sucking it up with these flights."

Antonor missed only one game at Florida State. It's only a one-hour flight to Tampa, so he makes it to all the home games. He's able to rent a car and drive to some of the Bucs road games. He's okay with flights of two hours or less.

He wants his son to be a role model, let others learn by his experiences, and "[make] sure kids see the positive in life and whatever they put their mind to they can accomplish," he said. "Jameis is in the spotlight now and is a role model whether he likes it or not. What you are going to do with that light on you is up to the individual now."

Winston is one of the brightest young stars in the NFL, playing for what has typically been one of the most unsuccessful franchises. It didn't take long for him to provide hope, improving from twenty-two touchdowns to twenty-eight touchdowns his first year to his second year as the Bucs' victory total increased from six victories in 2015 to nine in 2016, with Tampa staying alive in the play-off race until deep into the season.

When Winston visited the Bucs before the 2015 draft, Dirk Koetter was the offensive coordinator. He said Winston had the football IQ of a forty-five-year-old coach. He is that into football. By Winston's second season, Koetter was the head coach and Winston was all about trying to please him.

"It's the kind of relationship where you got a son that sees his dad working hard and all that son wants to do is try to continue to make his dad happy," Winston told the *Tampa Bay Times*. "That's what I'm doing. By me studying, me preparing, I'm making Coach Koetter happy in the big picture. Together, we're making this team get better."

Koetter said, "This kid is special. This kid is special and what he's done, forget dropping back and passes over the middle, what this guy has done as a leader and with the team at this age. It's impressive."

Even with Winston playing at a high level in the best football league in the world, his father is still his hardest and most effective critic. Jameis still listens to every word Ant says, but he has to believe, if even for a day, that if he were to win the Super Bowl, his father might take it easy on him.

"Honestly, that would be a day that he would probably tell me, 'I have nothing to say to you, son, great job,'" he said. "He would probably tell me to go watch film and see how I can get better. 'But today, we are going to celebrate. You are a Super Bowl champion.'"

Jaboo and Ant would then go out and celebrate together.

JOHN ELWAY
This One's for Dad

Jack Elway, the coach at San José State, charged off the sideline at Stanford Stadium to position himself within yelling distance of Stanford coach Paul Wiggin. Elway's defense was beating up Wiggins's quarterback, and Elway was not happy that the kid was still in the game. The quarterback was his kid.

John Elway was in his junior season and suffering through the worst day of his college career. His father felt his pain. It was the middle of the third quarter in September 1981, and Jack was unable to watch John absorb any more punishment. Not quite as important, but also on his mind, and a source of anxiety, was the hell he would catch from his wife, Janet, at dinner that night.

Jack Elway ventured all the way out to the numbers so Wiggin could hear him. John heard him, too.

"Get him out of there!" Elway screamed.

San José State was on its way to a 28–6 victory. Elway's son was playing on a sprained ankle and was an easy target, but he wouldn't come out of the game. Jack Elway was in his third year as coach of the Spartans, and his son had beaten him the first two times they met. The previous week, Elway had thrown for 418 yards in a season-opening loss to Purdue. The end result was the same against San José State, but the numbers were much different.

Elway completed just 6 of 24 passes for 72 yards. He was sacked seven times. He threw five interceptions, all in the second half. Stanford was held to fewer than 100 yards offense. John's mother watched in agony—she hated the Stanford–San José State games of father versus son—and cringed as John was getting pummeled. What mother enjoys watching her baby boy get beat up on the football field? Even more painful was the fact that her husband was coaching the team doing the punishing.

"Sure, I had mixed feelings," Jack Elway said after the game. "John is still the best quarterback I have ever seen. But he has a responsibility to his team, and I have a responsibility to my team."

Jack Elway realized he was going to have a lot of explaining to do to his wife when he arrived back home in San José. He put together a quick plan. After the game, he met John at midfield to first make sure he was still in one piece. Then he invited him to dinner.

"Are you going to come home to San José tonight?" Jack asked.

The drive from the Stanford campus, known as "The Farm," to the Elway house was an easy twenty miles south on the 101 Freeway. John made the trip all the time. It's hard to beat one of Mom's home-cooked meals when you're in college.

"No, I'm going to hang at the dorm and stay up here," John said.

"I really want you to come home," Jack countered.

"I just really want to stay up here," John said.

He was more than a little curious why his father was so insistent. He had played an awful game; his team was 0-2; he was upset and banged up and just wanted to hang out with his buddies. As much as he loved his parents and enjoyed their company and talking football with his father, he wasn't in the mood.

"Okay, I'm not asking anymore. I'm telling you that you are going to come home to San José," Jack said.

"Why?" John finally asked.

"Because if you're not with me, your mom won't let me in the house," Jack said.

John went home.

It turned into an eventful evening. John had been drafted by the Yankees with the last pick in the second round of the 1981 draft in June—six spots ahead of future Hall of Fame out-fielder Tony Gwynn—and had been talking to them about an arrangement to play baseball in his time off from football while he was still at Stanford. He had his mind made up to play in the NFL—he was regarded as the best quarterback prospect of all time—but baseball had always been his first love. He signed a contract for $140,000 with the Yankees the night of the San José State game that would allow him to play baseball in the summer for New York's Class A minor-league team in Oneonta and return to play his senior year of football at Stanford. Elway was a right fielder with a rocket arm and a lot of potential. His plan all along was to play football, but where else was he going to find a summer job for $140,000? He later used the Yankees as leverage when the Baltimore Colts drafted him number 1 overall in 1983 against his wishes and he threatened to go play for George Steinbrenner instead of Robert Irsay. One week after the draft, the Colts traded Elway to the Denver Broncos.

Jack and John Elway were not only father and son, they were best friends. Jack was a major influence in John's decision not to play in Baltimore, just as he was responsible for his son's going out for quarterback instead of running back on his high school team. Elway had a magical arm, the strongest and most powerful in college football and later NFL history. On the first day of practice his freshman year at Stanford, he threw passes with such velocity that he broke the fingers of two of his receivers. It worked out a little better when his receivers chose to bring the ball into their bodies instead of catching it out front with their hands. Elway's passes arrived with such force that the nose of the football left a visible imprint on his receivers' chests. It became known as the Elway Cross, a proud if painful badge of honor.

Rod Smith, who didn't start catching passes from Elway until Elway's twelfth year in the NFL, said the Broncos coaches used to dial up the Jugs machine in practice to between 70 and 80 miles per hour to get them used to Elway's fastball. He knew only two speeds. Fast and faster.

"That cross in your chest?" Smith said. "I got a few of those from John."

Elway was a pitcher in Little League, which was the first time Jack Elway noticed something special about his only son's right arm. He could really throw hard. But in football, he liked to play running back. Throwing a football is not at all like throwing a baseball, and Elway was a faster runner than all the other kids. He liked getting the handoff and running all out.

Jack Elway was a teacher and football coach at Port Angeles High School in the state of Washington when John was born in 1959. Jack moved up to Grays Harbor College in Aberdeen, Washington, in 1961 and remained there until he began the nomadic life of a college assistant coach. The family settled in Missoula, Montana, in 1966 when Jack was hired as an assistant coach at the University of Montana. John began playing Pop Warner football and loved it. But when Jack was hired as an assistant at Washington State in 1972, football was not a part of John's life. There was no Pop Warner program.

"So I really didn't play again until ninth grade," Elway said.

Jack was driving John to class on the first day of high school football practice. They both knew this was the year he would start playing serious football.

"Well, football starts today," Jack said.

"Yeah, it starts today," John said.

"What position you going out for?" Jack asked.

"Well, I'm planning on going out for running back," John said.

The high school played the old single wing, created by Glenn "Pop" Warner. It was a running offense with four backs in the backfield.

Jack was driving a '68 Chevy Impala, a model with the gear-shift on the steering wheel. Jack Elway put the car in park. John wondered why they were stopping short of the school. Jack saw his son as a quarterback, not a running back. They sat in the car and discussed the only option Jack was giving him. Mainly, John listened. Jack knew his son had a golden arm. "I want you to play quarterback," Jack said. "But I want to play running back," John said. They went back and forth for what seemed like forever.

"Fifteen minutes later I got out of the car and I'm a quarterback," John said, laughing. "I tried to talk him out of it. The single-wing offense was pretty boring. Having been a running back, I like to carry the ball. I like to be in on the action. But I knew I was starting to grow and I didn't have the speed I had when I was in fifth grade when I was faster than everybody else. I started growing and things started slowing down a little bit, especially my speed."

Father knows best. "In the long run, as time went on, this was going to be the position for me even though it might not have been the most fun," John said. "He told me I would be able to run the bootleg and do other stuff, too, in the single wing. In the long run, he said, the best thing for me was to go out for quarterback."

Elway played quarterback in the ninth grade, trying to get settled in at a new position. Jim Sweeney had hired Jack Elway for his staff at Washington State, but after a promising 7-4 record in their first season in 1972, the Cougars regressed with records of 5-6, 2-9, and 3-8 the next three years. Sweeney was fired. Elway lost his job. John lost his football team.

Jack Elway was hired as an assistant at Cal State–Northridge in the San Fernando Valley. He moved ahead of his wife and three children to buy a house and get settled. The kids finished out the school year. It was important to find a home in an area that had a good football program to allow John to reach his potential. He picked Granada Hills. The coach was Jack Neumeier, who had won city and state titles.

"They threw the ball all over," John Elway said. "He was way ahead of his time. My sophomore year is where I really started enjoying the position because I did get to throw it all over the place."

Elway didn't have a lot of experience at quarterback. But he grew up fast. He had the arm and was a perfect match for the offense. "I got a chance to throw it a lot," he said.

He quickly developed into a big-time college prospect at the same time Jack Elway's coaching career was about to take off. Jack was an offensive coach, and John really admired the system his father ran. They were as close as a father and son could be. Best friends, really. It was such an advantage for John to be able to come home from practice or a game and sit with his father and talk business. There are plenty of young men who go into the family business, but not often does it play out in front of the cameras or in the newspapers. But the Elways were different. One was a quarterback and the other was a coach.

After the 1978 season, Jack Elway was hired as the head coach at San José State, his first really big job. John Elway was one of the hottest quarterback recruits in the country. Of course, his father wanted his son to play for him. "He said, 'I can't offer cars or anything,' but he did offer to have an affair with my mother," John said.

Even though the NCAA has strict rules, that would not have been a violation.

It could have been an uncomfortable period in their lives. John started dreaming about playing in the Pac-10 Conference when his father was coaching at Washington State. He loved the style of play, the wide-open offense. In his mind, before his father was hired by San José State, he was going to decide between the University of Southern California and Stanford University. Excellent schools academically and great football programs.

His mother wanted him to go to Stanford. "I think deep down inside, my dad wanted me to go there, too, even though he'd love to have me play for him," Elway said.

His father did try his best to get John to join him. He had him up for a visit on campus. The coach didn't have to make a home visit. "He impressed my mom, let's put it that way," John said.

It was the identical situation Jim and Jack Harbaugh faced years later when Michigan wanted Jim in 1982 and Jack had just been named the head coach at Western Michigan. Jim went to Michigan to play for Bo Schembechler.

John Elway was torn. He wanted to go to Stanford. He had his heart set on Stanford. It is a great school with a football program that emerged under Bill Walsh, who left for the 49ers in 1979, the year Elway would arrive on campus. Wide receivers coach Rod Dowhower, a well-respected offensive mind, was promoted to replace Walsh. But if John went and played for his father and helped lead San José State's football program into national prominence, it could help elevate Jack into the spotlight, perhaps setting him up for an NFL head coaching job.

That's a heavy burden for an eighteen-year-old. But Jack never tried to appeal to John's heart. He tried to sell him on doing great things together: He would prepare his son to play in the NFL, and John could set him up for a coaching job at the next level if they won a lot of games. "I think he knew my mom wanted me to go to Stanford, too," John said. "He didn't want to push too hard."

Elway followed his football heart and went to Stanford. His dad understood.

Stanford won the first two games of the Elway-versus-Elway matchup, and San José State won the last two. Elway continued to lean on his father for advice on and off the field during his college days. "I'd always get an honest opinion from him and he didn't pull any punches," John said. "He wasn't overly negative ever, but if I had done something wrong or made a bad mistake, he would let me know that. You wanted to make your dad proud of you, especially when he was a football coach. If I could do that, then everything else was good."

Jack was not heavy-handed, never telling John what he needed to do better. He asked questions and let him figure it out for himself. "That's why, in my mind, he was a great football coach and he did a tremendous job when he was a coach," John said. "He was always asking me questions to get me where he wanted me to be."

Elway spent the summer between his junior and senior years playing baseball for the Yankees in Oneonta in upstate New York. The better Elway became in football, the more Yankees owner George Steinbrenner wanted to steal him away from the NFL to play baseball. What could be better for Steinbrenner than taking the best quarterback prospect in the history of college football and grooming him to be a right fielder for the New York Yankees? Elway had high-level baseball skills, and if he'd dedicated himself to the game, he might have made it to the Bronx.

He hit .342 in forty-two games for Oneonta and of course had a very strong arm. He could hit, hit with power, run, field, and throw: the five tools of baseball. If he became a full-time baseball player, he could fulfill his potential. "He will be a great outfielder for me, in the great tradition of Mantle, Maris, DiMaggio, and all the others," Steinbrenner once said.

Steinbrenner, as competitive as Elway, would have loved it if that taste of professional baseball in the summer of 1982 had provided enough of a temptation for Elway to turn his back on football. The coaches and players around the Oneonta Yankees knew he had excellent baseball skills, but they had also watched him play quarterback for Stanford, where he was a once-in-a-generation player. He had one more season of college football remaining when he played in Oneonta, and even though he was on the verge of becoming the first player picked in the 1983 NFL draft, he never big-timed his teammates. He never did that in the NFL, either. He always tried to just fit in and be one of the fellas.

He told *Yankees Magazine* that he really cherished his time with the minor-league team. "I enjoyed traveling on the buses, and we went to a local pizza parlor for dinner and a few beers after every home game, and that was always a great time," he said. "None of us had cars, so we walked to the park every day. We walked to the pizza parlor after the games and walked home after that. It was a great experience for me."

Elway never had to ride the buses from one city to the next in the NFL. But he enjoyed the life of a minor-league player for one summer, and when he ended his Oneonta summer on a hot streak, he was convinced he could make it to the major leagues if he stuck with it.

"Finishing the season the way I did gave me a lot of confidence that I could play baseball at a high level," Elway said to *Yankees Magazine*. "I was going right into my senior football season and I was really looking forward to that. But baseball had become a viable option for me that summer. I enjoyed playing baseball every day and I was confident because I had some success. I left there thinking, 'I don't know what's going to happen, but this is something I would definitely be happy doing for a long time.'"

Elway was a two-sport star before Deion Sanders and Bo Jackson, who each played in the NFL and Major League Baseball at the same time. Sanders is the only player to have played in both the World Series and the Super Bowl. In 1992, Sanders played in a Saturday night National League Championship Series game with the Atlanta Braves in Pittsburgh, flew to Miami and played for the Falcons on Sunday afternoon, and then returned to Pittsburgh for Game 5 of the Series against the Pirates, although he didn't play.

Jackson played baseball in the same season with the Los Angeles Raiders and the Kansas City Royals from 1987 to 1990 before a hip injury ended his football career. Jackson was the first player picked in the 1986 draft by the Buccaneers but stunned the NFL when he elected to play baseball and never signed with Tampa. He was picked by the Los Angeles Raiders in the fifth round in 1987 and worked out a deal to join them after baseball season was over.

As much as John Elway loved baseball, he had learned to love football even more. He was a transcendent talent. In baseball, he had potential. In football, he was a sure thing.

After spending the summer with Oneonta, he returned for his senior season. His Stanford team once again lost to his father, Jack, and San José State, this time 35–31. Stanford was just 5-6, but Elway won the Sammy Baugh Award as the nation's top college quarterback.

Elway went into the 1983 NFL draft process as the consensus overall number 1 pick and was considered the best quarterback prospect of all time. His arm strength was already legendary; he was athletic and could throw on the run; he could even unleash a bullet running to his right and throwing across his body to his left. He had a great aptitude for the game, and, despite his talent, he did not have a big head and was considered a good kid. Having a father who was a longtime football coach made him an even more attractive prospect. Football was important to him.

||||||||||||||||||||||||||||||||||||||||||||

By the end of the 1982 college football season, it became evident that the next draft was going to be outstanding for quarterbacks. Elway; Jim Kelly (Miami); Dan Marino (Pittsburgh); Todd Blackledge (Penn State); and Tony Eason (Illinois) were all considered locks for the first round. Surprisingly, they were joined by Ken O'Brien from little-known Cal-Davis, who wound up getting drafted by the Jets over Marino, who had a poor senior season and whose value plummeted because of drug use rumors.

There was no doubt that Elway was the best quarterback in the group. The Baltimore Colts had the first pick, but just one year earlier they had selected Ohio State quarterback Art Schlichter with the fourth overall selection. Could they take a quarterback even higher after Schlichter's rookie season? The Colts finished a league-worst 0-8-1 in the 1982 strike-shortened season. Schlichter threw only 37 passes in three games and didn't make one start. It would be foolish to think his presence would convince Ernie Accorsi, the first-year Colts general manager, to pass on Elway. Accorsi learned the value of franchise quarterbacks in his years in Baltimore with Johnny Unitas. He had been promoted from assistant general manager to general manager by Colts owner Robert Irsay and wasn't about to trade the pick or take another player, even though future Hall of Fame running back Eric Dickerson was available in the draft.

Accorsi was locked in on Elway. But there was a problem. Elway didn't want to play for Baltimore. He didn't have any negative feelings about the city of Baltimore, but his father, Jack, didn't want him playing for Irsay, a heavy drinker who was not held in high regard in the NFL, or for Frank Kush, a rigid taskmaster who had been hired as the Colts coach in 1982 and proceeded to go winless. Kush had recruited Elway to play for him when he was the coach at Arizona State, but Elway didn't even take a trip to Tempe to visit.

Elway told the Colts not to draft him. He threatened to play baseball for the Yankees. He was portrayed as an entitled kid who thought he was bigger than the draft, bigger than the NFL, as he attempted to dictate where he would play.

He had little desire to play for Kush, but it was more about the Colts organization. He didn't know much about Accorsi, a former newspaper reporter who had worked for the *Charlotte News*, the *Baltimore Sun*, and the *Philadelphia Inquirer* and once broke the story that the Philadelphia 76ers traded Wilt Chamberlain to the Los Angeles Lakers. Accorsi was from Hershey, Pennsylvania, and his father attended Chamberlain's 100-point game in Hershey in 1962. Accorsi worked his way up in the NFL from public relations to general manager, and even though he went on to be one of the best general managers of his generation, and in 2016 was inducted into the Ring of Honor of the New York Giants, he had yet to establish a track record.

Irsay became an NFL owner in 1972 when he bought the Los Angeles Rams from the estate of the late Dan Reeves—no relation to the former Dallas Cowboys running back who was later the head coach of three NFL teams—and on the same day swapped franchises with Colts owner Carroll Rosenbloom. Irsay wasn't known as much of a football man. He made his money in the family's HVAC business. When Irsay died in 1997, the obituary written by the Associated Press described him as a "meddlesome, tightfisted tyrant in Baltimore." The *Baltimore Sun* remembered him for his "drunken fits of rage."

The Elways did their homework on Irsay and the Colts. Accorsi did his homework on Elway. The Elways made it clear to the Colts that John did not want to play for them. Accorsi made it clear to them that he would not be intimidated and would not trade the choice unless he received three first-round draft picks. He would never pass on Elway and take another player just because Elway said he didn't want to play for the Colts.

"It's the most influential position in football and probably in sports," Accorsi once said. "Maybe the Wilt Chamberlain, Bill Russell, Kareem Abdul-Jabbar era, when the center dominated so much, was just as important."

Accorsi is a historian. He wasn't about to be remembered as the man who panicked and gave away Elway without getting equal return. Besides, what leverage did Elway really have? The Yankees? He didn't want to play baseball. Sitting out the season and entering the 1984 draft? He would lose a year off his career. Neither were attractive options.

"It really came down to 'How solid is this organization?' It was really Irsay and it was unstable in what they were doing," Elway said. "They drafted a quarterback the year before and there had been no direction in what they were doing. It was mainly, looking in the long run, was I going to have a chance to be successful? Is this going to give me the best chance at being successful in football by going to the Baltimore Colts or not? We looked at it and we didn't think so. The ownership was unstable and they would make decisions on the fly."

Elway would clash with Broncos coach Dan Reeves when they were together in Denver for the first ten years of Elway's career. Reeves is a pussycat compared to Kush. "Frank Kush was not my dad's style, but he was not the main reason," Elway said. "If it had been a solid organization, if it was the Denver Broncos and Frank Kush was the coach, I'd have come here."

That conflicted with the information Accorsi received years later when he was the Giants assistant general manager and Jim Fassel was hired by George Young as the head coach. Fassel was Elway's offensive coordinator at Stanford and they were very good friends. So good, in fact, that Fassel was in John Elway's wedding party when he married his first wife, Janet, after his rookie season.

Fassel told Accorsi that Kush was the reason Elway didn't want to play for the Colts. The information came from Elway. It was probably a combination of two things: John Elway was scared of Irsay, and Jack Elway was scared of Kush. Elway said he always regretted blaming geography.

"We kind of came up with the lame excuse that we wanted to stay on the West Coast and that ended up backfiring," he said.

To people on the East Coast, Denver is the West Coast.

Elway laughed. "They don't realize it snows here."

Marvin Demoff was one of the most powerful agents in football. He represented Elway and Marino in the 1983 draft.

At the NFL owners meetings in Palm Springs, California, one month before the draft, Demoff arranged a dinner with Jack Elway, Accorsi, and Kush. They dined in the hotel restaurant.

"The purpose of the meeting was not to talk about the possibility of us drafting him," Accorsi said. "They wanted to express in person that John didn't want to get drafted by the Colts."

Accorsi knew Demoff well. They had done many contracts over the years. Even before dinner, Accorsi heard the rumors that Elway didn't want the Colts to pick him.

"Dinner was very low-key. It was done very professionally," Accorsi said.

Jack Elway was quiet. He let Demoff do the talking.

Accorsi wanted Elway, but he had a backup plan. Even though Marino's stock was slipping, if Accorsi could come up with a record-setting haul for Elway, he would make the trade if he could still get Marino. He wanted three first-round picks, with two in one year, and two second-round picks.

Elway and his father came up with a list of ten teams that he would accept a trade to. The Cowboys were interested, and Accorsi asked for Randy White and Danny White and two first-round picks. Tom Landry, Tex Schramm, and Gil Brandt refused. San Diego had three first-round picks in the 1983 draft—the fifth, twentieth, and twenty-second—but were not willing to part with the best of the three. No deal. The Raiders were trying to acquire the Bears' pick at number 6 to go along with their own pick at number 26 and would have traded both to Baltimore. But Chicago wanted Howie Long from the Raiders and the talks died. If the deal had gone through, Accorsi was going to take Marino in the Bears' slot.

The Patriots called Irsay and offered All-Pro guard John Hannah and the fifteenth pick in the first round in exchange for the first spot. Irsay wanted to do the deal. Accorsi threatened to quit.

The draft started at 7 a.m. Each team had fifteen minutes to make its first-round choice. No acceptable offer had been made to Accorsi. He told Irsay he was going to select Elway at one second after seven. Irsay was overheard telling team counsel Michael Chernoff that he would allow Accorsi to have his moment of glory by taking Elway, but then he would take over and trade Elway.

Three days after the draft, Elway called Accorsi to apologize. He wasn't backtracking on his decision not to play in Baltimore. He apologized for embarrassing Accorsi, knowing his refusal to play for the Colts was a bad reflection on him, but the decision had nothing to do with Accorsi. Accorsi appreciated the phone call, but he was not budging. You want to go play baseball, go play baseball.

He had checked with sources he had in baseball and acquired Elway's scouting report. "He wasn't really a major-league prospect," Accorsi said. "I figured on July 15 when he's hitting .260 and riding the bus in Greensboro that he would want to play football."

This was business. It was also Accorsi's first draft. He did not hire Kush. He did not pick Schlichter one year earlier. In fact, he didn't want him. "I was against that pick," he said. "That was Irsay."

Accorsi had gotten word that Elway was looking for a five-year $5 million contract. He made the mistake of telling Irsay. If Accorsi had any chance to keep Elway and call his baseball bluff...that ended it. There was no chance Irsay was going to pay that kind of money.

Irsay was an impossible owner, and Accorsi knew staying in that job could ruin his NFL career. But for now, the best way to protect himself was to protect the franchise. Ten days after the draft, Accorsi was sitting at home watching the NBA playoffs when ESPN interrupted the game with breaking news. The network teased it by saying there had been a big quarterback trade. Accorsi sat up. "Wonder what happened," he was thinking. He then found out that Irsay had run an end around on him and traded Elway to Denver for tackle Chris Hinton, who had been picked three spots after Elway; the Broncos' first-round pick in 1984 (subsequently used to pick guard Ron Solt); and backup quarterback Mark Herrmann. In addition, Broncos owner Edgar Kaiser agreed to host the Colts in preseason games at Mile High Stadium in 1984 and 1985. The gate receipts were split fifty-fifty between the home and visiting teams. The Broncos always drew a full house in the preseason, and receipts from the two games would put $800,000 in Irsay's bank account.

Elway had to deal with the criticism that he was spoiled and a crybaby. He wanted to play where he wanted to play, and his talent gave him the leverage. But it came with a price. Elway's image was being damaged.

Irsay had gone over Accorsi's head and behind his back and was dealing directly with the owners of the other franchises. Reeves had inquired about trading for the Colts' pick before the draft, but the price was too high. Denver knew that the Colts liked Hinton, so they had a valuable asset. If Irsay had forced the trade on Accorsi before the draft, he would have taken Marino. Instead, he had an offensive tackle, a backup quarterback, and a future first-round pick.

After the 1983 season, Accorsi quit and was hired by Art Modell in Cleveland as the Browns general manager. Following the 1986, 1987, and 1989 seasons, Elway's Broncos beat Accorsi's Browns in the AFC Championship Game. When Accorsi joined the Giants in 1994, it was Dan Reeves's second year as coach of Big Blue after he had been fired in Denver, primarily because of a fractured relationship with Elway.

John Elway was hired by the Broncos to run their football operations late in the 2011 season. Once the season ended, he began a search for a new head coach. He retained Accorsi as a consultant.

Perhaps he felt he owed him one. Accorsi recommended former Panthers coach John Fox, who had been the Giants' defensive coordinator when he was the Giants' general manager. Elway hired Fox, who helped Denver make it to one Super Bowl.

|||||||||||||||||||||||||||||||||||||||||||||||||

John Elway retired as a player with Super Bowl rings earned in the final two years of his sixteen-year career. He had the greatest exit in NFL history. Even though he had incredible talent, great success did not come easily in Denver. Elway lost three Super Bowls in his first seven seasons to the Giants, Redskins, and 49ers by a combined score of 136–40. Each loss was worse than the one that preceded it. It started with a 39–20 loss to the Giants, then 42–10 the next year to the Redskins, and 55–10 two years later to the 49ers. His 98-yard drive in the final minutes of the 1986 AFC Championship Game in Cleveland, which became known as "The Drive," sent the game into overtime, which the Broncos won. It might have been the greatest under-pressure drive in NFL history, but there would be no doubt about it if the Broncos had gone on to win the Super Bowl.

Reeves's philosophy with those Broncos teams was to keep the score close until the fourth quarter and then ask Elway to win it. It worked in the AFC, the much weaker conference at the time. Reeves never gave Elway the defense that Elway gave Peyton Manning when Manning played the last four years of his career with the Broncos, and Reeves never gave him a running game. Elway resented Reeves as a person and his approach as a coach. Even though he was all but a one-man team in his first three Super Bowls, he was the face of the franchise and received a majority of the criticism.

It reached the point in Denver where Broncos fans were actually afraid of their team getting back to the Super Bowl. They almost preferred losing in an earlier round, or not making the play-offs at all, to being subjected to further humiliation.

Elway turned to his family for comfort. He wasn't getting

any from Reeves. After their first year or two, the Elway-Reeves relationship deteriorated. Elway resented that Reeves played conservatively for three quarters and then put the pressure on Elway to win the game, rather than turning him loose earlier. It would gradually get worse between Elway and Reeves, who in their final couple of years together came to believe that his quarterback and offensive coordinator Mike Shanahan were conspiring behind his back.

John was always close to his twin sister, Jana, who died of cancer in 2002 at the age of forty-two. He had his first wife, Janet, to lean on, although they later divorced in December 2003. But the one person who really understood what he was going through on the football field was his father, Jack.

"He was a support system for me, not so much on the field, but mentally and off the field," John said. "He encouraged me to stay in there and keep working hard and try to put things behind you and keep the focus forward."

Jack's success at San José State led him to Stanford, John's school, when he was hired as head coach in 1984, two seasons after his son left. Jack coached Stanford for five seasons before he was fired and finished up his coaching career with the Frankfurt Galaxy of the World League of American Football.

The Super Bowl losses were hard on John. "I always leaned on my father," Elway said. "He was always that sounding board and especially because Dan and I didn't get along very well a lot of the time."

The three losses in the Super Bowl were hard on Jack as well. His son was getting blamed. Terry Bradshaw, a four-time

Super Bowl champion, was critical of Elway. Of course, Bradshaw was surrounded by a team of future Hall of Famers when he won his championships. Elway never had that kind of talent around him in Denver. Through it all, John knew Jack would always be there to say the right thing.

"He was just as disappointed, if not more disappointed, than I was after the Super Bowl losses," John said. "Having kids now, I know how disappointed I was when my kids have lost games."

Jack Elway tried to help John work on his relationship with Reeves. It had turned into a nightmare, and at one point Reeves considered trading Elway to his friend Joe Gibbs in Washington. Elway was miserable playing for Reeves. Even though Marino was not having the same team success as Elway, he was putting up huge numbers playing for Don Shula. Elway looked at the records Marino was setting and could only dream about what he could do playing for a coach who let him be himself the entire four quarters rather than being ultraconservative for three quarters before putting it all on him.

If the ultimate goal is winning championships, then Shula failed Marino just as Reeves failed Elway. Marino made it to the Super Bowl in his second season in 1984, the year he set records with 48 touchdown passes and 5,084 yards passing. The Dolphins lost 38–16 to Joe Montana and the 49ers, and Marino never made it back to the Super Bowl in the final fifteen years of his career. Marino had the numbers. Elway had the Super Bowl appearances. They were both unfulfilled until Elway won two titles with Shanahan as his coach.

Jack Elway attempted to help John understand Reeves. Not from an Xs and Os standpoint but in how he was handling him. The Elways had been afraid of Kush, but now John was having issues with Reeves, a stubborn and old-fashioned coach who was a disciple of Tom Landry.

"He did give me the head coach's viewpoint from the other side to try to help me understand," John said.

What could Jack say after the three Super Bowls to make John feel better? The message was not to give up. "He would never let us quit anything," Elway said. "If you start it, you're going to finish it no matter what it was. He'd always say, 'Be wise before you start something because if you start it, you're going to finish it. Make sure you have good information before you start it and it's something you want to do.'"

Elway never thought of quitting, even if there is nothing worse in football than losing the Super Bowl. One game, all or nothing; every mistake is magnified. The further a team advances in the NFL play-offs, the harder it is to accept defeat. Elway had to deal with three blowout losses.

Elway quit on one of his teams only once. He was wrestling in high school.

He went to his father and told him that he "couldn't stand kids sweating on me," he said.

Jack broke his own rule. He let his son off the hook.

"Just understand, this is the only time I'm ever going to let you quit anything," he said.

That was Jack's mentality. Start it. Finish it.

"Once we got through those three Super Bowl losses, they

got more discouraging as they went on," Elway said. "I was like, 'Okay, we dug ourselves a hole.' Now we've just got to figure out how to get to the next level and that's to win one. His mentality was instead of looking backward about what went wrong, try to find a solution to make it right."

||||||||||||||||||||||||||||||||||||||||||||

Elway and the Broncos were 11-point underdogs to Brett Favre and the defending champion Packers when they met in Super Bowl XXXII in San Diego. By then, Elway was in his sixteenth season and was the sentimental favorite. The Broncos had last been in the Super Bowl eight years earlier. Elway had a crazy run for a first down in the third quarter—later named "the Helicopter" because he went flying after giving up his body—that set up a key Broncos touchdown.

Elway was helped in the final two minutes when Packers coach Mike Holmgren made a crucial miscalculation. He lost track of downs. The score was tied at 24 when Denver moved to a first-and-goal situation at the Green Bay 8-yard line with two minutes remaining. The Packers had two of their time-outs remaining.

On first down, Super Bowl MVP Terrell Davis ran 7 yards, but tight end Shannon Sharpe was called for holding. It sent Denver back to the 18. Davis then ran 17 yards to the 1, setting up second down. Holmgren thought Davis had picked up a first down, forgetting the penalty had made it first and goal from the 17 rather than first and 10 from the 17. He thought the Broncos, at the very least, would run down the clock and kick the game-winning field goal without allowing Brett Favre much time to send the game into overtime. He instructed the Green Bay defense to part like the Red Sea and allow Davis to score. In fact, if he was aware it was second down and not first down, he could have used his final time-outs after the second and the third downs and left Favre enough time to try to get the Packers into position for the tying field goal. Of course, that was all contingent on the Green Bay defense being able to keep the Broncos out of the end zone, which was unlikely but not impossible.

Holmgren's strategy put the ball back into Favre's hands at his own 30 with 1:39 remaining and two time-outs. He was able to advance the Packers to the Broncos' 31 with 42 seconds left on the clock, but his fourth-down pass to Mark Chmura fell incomplete.

The Broncos offense came onto the field and Elway executed the sweetest kneel down of his career. NFL commissioner Paul Tagliabue handed the Lombardi Trophy to Broncos owner Pat Bowlen, who held the trophy in his hand and shouted, "This one's for John!"

Elway was overcome with joy. He had finally won the big game. The critics, led by Terry Bradshaw, could keep quiet now. He had just beaten Favre, who by then was the best and most dangerous quarterback in the league. He had received a lot of help from Davis, who rushed for 157 yards and three touchdowns despite a debilitating migraine headache. The pain reached such unbearable levels that Davis was unable to see clearly and was at times put in as a decoy in the first half to occupy the Green Bay defense. He went into the locker room to take his migraine medication, and the extra minutes tacked onto halftime for the entertainment allowed the medication to work so he was able to come out and play the second half. Davis was the biggest difference between Elway's losing his first three Super Bowls and finally winning in his fourth attempt. That game is a major reason Davis was elected in 2017 to join Elway in the Pro Football Hall of Fame.

John Elway sought out his father, Jack, in the cramped Broncos locker room underneath the stands at the dilapidated Qualcomm Stadium. Equipment bags and shoulder pads and sweaty uniforms and an overflow crowd of media—the usual locker-room scene—made navigating hard, but John found his father and they shared a long embrace.

"Look, Dad. Finally. We finally got it done!" John said.

Jack Elway's coaching career was over. He had been hired by the Broncos as a scout in 1993 and the next year became the director of pro scouting, having input into signing veteran free agents. They were able to share the moment and earn a Super Bowl ring. Knowing his father played a part in his first championship meant so much to Elway.

"It was worth the wait to be able to do it together," John Elway said.

The Broncos won the Super Bowl again the following year, starting the season 14-0, threatening to be the first team to put together a 16-0 regular season. But John's old friend Jim Fassel and the Giants beat the Broncos in a last-second thriller to give

Denver its first loss. It was an injury-plagued season for Elway. All the bumps and bruises, the surgeries, the big hits, took their toll. He missed three games during the regular season. But he ended his career in style, throwing for 336 yards in the Broncos' 34–19 victory over the Falcons. He was named Super Bowl MVP. Three months later, he announced his retirement.

Jack Elway died from a heart attack on April 15, 2001. He was no longer working full-time for the Broncos, but he sat in on draft meetings. John asked Shanahan if it would be okay if he was present for those meetings as well. He was out of football at the time, but observing the draft preparation would be helpful as he prepared for a career in the front office. He didn't know at the time that it would be the last quality time he would ever spend with his father, who was only sixty-nine years old when he died. John cherished being with his father in those meetings until he passed away two weeks before the draft at his home in Palm Springs.

"I got to sit next to my dad every single day. I enjoyed that time," John said. "We really got a chance to sit down and talk about personnel and evaluation. He was a very good personnel man. So I got a chance to hear some of his anecdotes about what he liked and what he didn't like. When I was playing, it was so much about my career that we never ever had a chance to talk about football as a whole. I really started to pick his brain and get deeper into it, but then he passed away."

John Elway became the CEO and part owner of the Colorado Crush of the Arena Football League in 2003. He was out of football again when the league folded after the 2008 season, but in 2011 Bowlen asked him to come back and run the Broncos as general manager and executive vice president of football operations. His first big move in 2012 was taking a chance on Peyton Manning, who had been released by the Colts after his fourth neck operation in two years. Manning picked the Broncos over the 49ers and Titans. Elway was one of the major reasons. Why? He did a great sales job from one quarterback to another. Elway convinced Manning that he would be able to surround him with a solid defense and quality skill-position players who would give him the best chance to succeed.

The Broncos made the play-offs all four years they had Manning. In his second season, Denver lost to Seattle 43–8 in Super Bowl XLVIII at MetLife Stadium in East Rutherford, New Jersey, a loss as humiliating as any of the three Elway suffered as a player. In the final game of Manning's career, the Broncos beat the Panthers 24–10, in Super Bowl 50 (the only Super Bowl with an arabic number rather than a roman numeral). He was not nearly the player Elway was at the end of his career, but Elway's shrewd personnel moves allowed Manning to go out a winner, just as Elway had done following Manning's rookie year in 1998.

When the Broncos won the Super Bowl with Elway as the architect of the team, John held up the trophy and shouted, "This one's for Pat!" as a tribute to Broncos owner Pat Bowlen, who was suffering from Alzheimer's and unable to attend the game. Elway could have easily said, "And this one's also for Dad."

Elway thought of his father and how he would have felt about John's winning a title as an executive. "I think he would have been as proud, if not even more proud, than when I was a player, just because the influence he had on me in this area was really more than he did as a football player," Elway said. "Football was talent and the systems I was in, but this was more up his alley of what he did as a career coach and then being on the personnel side. I'm glad he held on for those Super Bowl wins. I just feel like I was so lucky to have him for as long as I had him."

John thinks about Jack all the time. He misses him a lot. "What would Jack do?" John said. "I always think about what I could have learned from him. Also, I feel bad. I know he would have been my right-hand man, if he was still around, in the position I am in."

Elway waited the minimum five years before he was inducted into the Pro Football Hall of Fame in 2004. He was selected five years to the day after his final game. It hurt him deeply that Jana and Jack were both gone. "It puts life in perspective. We do the best we can," he said. "The thing my sister always said, one of the last things she said to me, she just wanted to live."

He spoke lovingly about his twin sister and about his dad at the induction ceremony in Canton, Ohio, on August 8, 2004.

"My dad wasn't just my best friend, he was my hero, my mentor, and my inspiration. He was the keeper of my reality checklist, and the compass that guided my life and my career. And he taught me the number 1 lesson of my life: Always make your family proud. Now that he's gone, I thank God every day for letting him see the Broncos win those two Super Bowls.

"My dad didn't so much teach me how to play football, but why to play it. He taught me to compete, to never give up, to play every down like it's your last. He taught me to appreciate the game, to respect it, to play it like it was meant to be played. He taught me to enjoy my successes and learn from my failures. And above all, he told me, 'Make sure when you go out with your offensive linemen, you pick up the tab.'"

And propose a toast to his old man.

DEREK CARR

A Flashy New Carr

Derek Carr invited his family to his house in Danville, about twenty-five miles outside Oakland, two days before Christmas in 2016 to celebrate the holiday.

The Raiders were having a magical season, and Carr was an MVP candidate in just his third season. He had a game the next afternoon on Christmas Eve at home against the Indianapolis Colts and would be required to report to the team hotel the night before the game, making that Friday afternoon the best time for Carr and his wife, Heather, and their two young sons, his parents, and his brothers, nieces, and nephews to get together for an early dinner and to open presents.

The Carrs are a religious, tight-knit family. David, the oldest, was the first overall pick in the 2002 draft by the expansion Houston Texans. Darren, the middle of the three sons, was a defensive lineman at the University of Houston. Football fans got their first glimpse of Derek on David's draft weekend in New York when he attended many of the NFL's events and was by David's side when he walked onstage at Radio City Music Hall in New York after Commissioner Paul Tagliabue announced the Texans' pick. Derek had just turned eleven years old.

On the day before Christmas 2016, Derek rented a suite for his parents, his brothers, and all the kids to see him play against the Indianapolis Colts at home at the Oakland Coliseum. It was David's first time to see his brother play in person in the NFL. David had retired following the 2012 season. "It was packed full of family," Rodger Carr, the patriarch, said. "That was one of the presents from Derek. We were all up there."

Carr, drafted near the top of the second round by the Raiders in 2014, had guided Oakland to an 11-3 record. They were in control of the AFC West and still had a chance to upend the Patriots and earn the top play-off seed in the AFC. That would be a considerable accomplishment. The Raiders had not been in the play-offs, or even finished over .500, since they were in the Super Bowl in 2002. In fact, they were an abysmal 63-145 from 2003 to 2015. But general manager Reggie McKenzie had drafted well and built the team around Carr and linebacker Khalil Mack, who was a pass-rushing force, and the eeriness of playing in the Black Hole gave this talented Raiders team a decided home field advantage.

Then came agony and shattered Super Bowl dreams.

There was 11:07 remaining in the fourth quarter against the Colts. The Raiders held a comfortable 33–14 lead. Run the ball, try to pick up some clock-killing first downs, don't get anybody hurt, and get the heck out of there. That should have been Oakland's approach. Carr instead dropped back to pass and wound up in the hospital. He was moving around in the pocket when he was brought down by Trent Cole. His right leg got twisted. Carr knew right away it was bad. He grabbed his right leg and yelled, "It's broke, it's broke," again and again.

He's no doctor, but he knows his body. His right fibula was indeed broken. A few days later, he had season-ending surgery.

The despair of the Carr family filled the suite. One minute they were enjoying the food and drink and what seemed to be a lopsided victory, and the next moment Derek Carr's season was over just as he neared the finish line.

"I read his lips, 'It's broke, it's broke, it's broke,' " Rodger Carr said. "All of us started crying. You know the work he put in to get to that point. We were in shock; Heather and my wife were crying. All the girls were so upset."

The Raiders held on to beat the Colts 33–25.

Officials from the Raiders took Heather to the locker-room area to see Derek.

"Rodger, I've never seen anything like that," she said. "Big, grown men coming in and crying and hugging Derek and telling him they love him."

"They are just a good group of men," Rodger said.

The prognosis for Derek after surgery was excellent.

"It's a scary feeling," Carr said on a radio show on 95.7 in the Bay Area one week after surgery. "I've rolled ankles and torn ligaments, but to have something break was an eerie feeling. Everything got silent, with the buzz in the stadium. I couldn't hear a thing. All I could focus on was, 'This isn't right.' "

But instead of being able to move on, every time Rodger Carr turned on the television in the days and weeks after his son was injured, it seemed the play of Derek being injured was being shown on the screen.

"I can't watch it," he said. "It's hard to watch."

The Raiders started journeyman backup quarterback Matt McGloin in a season-ending loss to the Broncos that dropped the Raiders from first place in the AFC West to the number 1 wild-card team. McGloin suffered a shoulder injury in Denver, and rookie Connor Cook was forced to start the play-off game in Houston. He had thrown just 21 passes during the regular season, all in the final game after McGloin was injured. He was ineffective against the Texans, and a season that had been so promising just a couple of weeks earlier came to a quiet end. Derek Carr said watching the Denver game on television "ripped my heart out."

Rodger Carr knew Derek would get past this crushing moment and come back and resume his quest for the Super Bowl. Derek could count on one thing: His father would be there for support.

||||||||||||||||||||||||||||||||||||||||||||

Derek Carr receives a text message from his father before every game.

"Hey," he says. "I love you. Have fun."

He and his wife are at every one of Derek's home games. They live in Bakersfield, a four-hour drive from Oakland, so they load up the car and hit the highway.

Rodger Carr was an excellent basketball player. "Amazing player," Derek said. "He averaged over 30 points a game in high school. He was one of the best players in the state of California. He had a full ride to USC but his mom, for some reason, said, 'I can't let you go.' So he went to Cal State–Bakersfield and that's where he met my mom. Thank the Lord that happened."

Rodger Carr is six foot five and played at 230 pounds. Back in the '70s, that was a big shooting guard. He had a forty-inch-plus vertical jump. Derek has a picture of himself sitting on a friend's head and dunking a basketball looking down at his father. "I was playing back in the day when we wore short shorts," Rodger said.

After suffering a back injury when he was nineteen, doctors wanted to do surgery. Rodger refused and his career was over. "His coaches were begging him not to stop playing," Derek said. "He would have easily went on to the NBA and played. He's an all-around athlete. He ran in the Junior Olympics."

When Rodger turned fifty, he took his three sons to the park. "He just wanted to play basketball," Derek said. "He said, 'I want to be able to dunk at fifty.' He went up and slammed it."

Fourteen years later, after playing basketball, Derek couldn't believe what he was seeing.

"You put a basketball in his hands, he looks like he's twenty-four," he said. "Man, that is unreal."

Derek always wanted to play basketball. He goes into the gym and starts drilling threes from NBA range like Steph Curry.

"When I retire from the NFL, I'm going to try out for the Warriors," Derek said.

"Dude, you're going to be a little old. You're six-three. Just think of the point guards you are going to have to cover," Rodger said.

Once he injured his back, Rodger Carr knew basketball wasn't in his future and he needed to think about what he was going to do with his life. He went to work for Roger Penske's auto dealership in Bakersfield after college. He got married and started to raise a family. He would work long hours, but he always found the time to throw around the football, first with David, then Darren, then Derek. Even these days, with one son an NFL quarterback and another a former NFL quarterback and Darren the head coach at Bakersfield Christian High School, they'll be sitting around watching television, somebody will pick up a football, and then they're all in the backyard throwing it around.

Rodger was working hard to support his family at the dealership. He started out in sales and was promoted to finance manager; then, after Penske sold the dealership, he became sales manager and then general sales manager. He would often leave for work early in the morning, and by the time he finished his paperwork it would be ten or eleven before he got home at night. On the days he would get home at nine, the boys were already showered and in their pajamas when he would summon them outside to throw the ball around.

Mom would object because her sons were already cleaned up, but Rodger had a rule: If he was home in time, he wanted to work one hour a day with them. "Come on outside," he'd say.

So they would.

"My mom always said she raised four boys and my dad was one of them," Derek said.

He would attend football practice, and most of the time he was the only parent watching. But he would stay off to the side and never get in the way of the coaches. If the coaches felt the need to yell at one of his kids, he didn't want them holding back just because he was around. Once they got home from a game, Rodger always had just the right thing to say.

"He knew us so well, knew our mood," Derek said. "If we messed up, he knew we would be down. He picked out the one thing that we did right and was just encouraging us and lifting us. It was the same thing if I went 4-for-4 in a baseball game or if I scored 16 points and hit five threes in a basketball game or if I threw six touchdowns, if I was feeling kind of good, he would say, 'Hey, man, I'm so proud of you. That was so fun to watch.' He would always blow it up way out of proportion like you threw twelve touchdowns or scored 40 points. He would remember the one ground ball that you kind of bobbled and told you to keep your head down on it. He would always keep it in perspective for us, but at the same time, he would blow it up like we were the best thing ever if we did something good."

Rodger kept up with the latest techniques of playing quarterback from his conversations with David and Derek, but he was not an overbearing helicopter father who tried to influence his sons' coaches. He was as close to his three sons as any father could possibly be, but he knew where to draw the line. The backyard was his domain. The practice field belonged to the coaches.

Until the day David was drafted first overall by the expansion Texans, the Carrs' family life was similar to that of so many others. But it all changed when David was taken by Texans general manager Charley Casserly to be their franchise quarterback. Casserly had been hired by Texans owner Bob McNair in 2000, two years before the team would take the field. Casserly spent twenty-three years with the Washington Redskins, first as an unpaid intern in 1977 to Coach George Allen, then as a scout, then as an assistant to General Manager Bobby Beathard in 1982, and then he was promoted to replace Beathard in 1989.

During his time with the Redskins, they won three Super Bowls. Hall of Famer Joe Gibbs was the coach, but each time Washington had a different starting quarterback: Joe Theismann in 1982, Doug Williams in 1987, and Mark Rypien in 1991. None of them were close to being Hall of Fame players, but the success spoke to the greatness of Gibbs and the ability of Beathard and Casserly to build the team with great complementary players.

Casserly is very thorough and methodical in his approach. He did his homework on how to start a team from scratch and hired Dom Capers as his coach. Capers had been the first coach of the expansion Carolina Panthers in 1995 and had them in the NFC Championship Game in their second season. Capers's quarterback in Carolina was Kerry Collins, who was the Panthers' first-round pick in their initial draft in 1995. He was taken fifth overall.

David Carr was a strong-armed quarterback from Fresno State. He was the consensus best quarterback in the draft ahead of Oregon's Joey Harrington, who was taken third by the Detroit Lions. North Carolina defensive end Julius Peppers was the best overall player in the draft and as a pass rusher had become the second-most-important player on the field. Quarterback was first. Casserly decided on Carr to become the face of the first-year franchise. It was the second time Casserly had selected a quarterback in the first round. Back in Washington in 1994, he made Tennessee's Heath Shuler the third overall pick, but that didn't turn out well. As long as Casserly could put together an offensive line to protect Carr, the team and the quarterback could grow together.

When the Texans drafted Carr, they really drafted the entire Carr family.

David and his wife, Melody, already had a baby boy, Austin. His brother Darren was playing at the University of Houston. Rodger and his wife, Sheryl, at David's urging, decided to move with Derek to Houston as well. Of course, Derek, who was too young to have been entrenched in any of his athletic teams, was thrilled at the idea of being around his big brothers, one playing in the NFL and the other playing in a big-time college program. David had signed a six-year $42 million contract, so Rodger was able to give up his job in the car dealership and assist his oldest son in his business affairs, and with his wife they were able to babysit for their grandson.

It was an unusual decision made by the family. It's not out of the ordinary for nineteen-year-old kids who leave college after one year for the NBA to bring in their big brothers to live with them and provide companionship during their rookie year. In some cases, moms are enlisted to help in the transition. Eli Manning had his mother help him set up his apartment in Hoboken, New Jersey, when he was a rookie before he was married. David Carr had a wife and a young son, but this is a family with such a strong bond that they all wanted to stay together.

"Oh my goodness, it was so cool to me," Derek said.

David was his hero, his mentor, his role model. He was, in effect, his football father.

Derek wanted the life that David had made for himself.

"Ever since I was five or six years old, I could throw a football better than people who were eleven or twelve years old," Derek said.

David would come home to Bakersfield from breaks in college, and he and Derek would go out in the street to throw the football around.

"David, watch him throw the ball," Rodger said.

Derek would let one loose.

"Dude, how old are you?" David said.

"Eight," Derek said.

David took Derek under his wing. He wanted to be there for him growing up. The age difference was going to make that tough once David went into the NFL. He was almost twenty-three when he was drafted. The kid brother was just past eleven years old. "David really wanted to be part of my middle school and high school career," Derek said. "He just wanted to be there to teach me and help me. He said, 'What better way for a young kid with talent to learn to really live the NFL life than with me?' I was David's biggest fan. I could just stay and hang out with my brother all the time now. In college, he was out in Fresno so I didn't get to see him all the time."

David had a rocket arm. Even at a young age, so did Derek. "I was so young, but I could throw the ball harder than people twice my age," Derek said. "They always told me I was like mini-Favre or Little Favre."

Brett Favre is why Derek Carr wears number 4 with the Raiders. "I'd never seen anybody throw a ball like him," Derek said. "I never really watched him play until I was maybe eight years old. He had a cannon. I'd never seen anybody throw the ball that hard."

He loved watching Favre. He admired how he took chances and gave his receivers the opportunity to make plays. "I just loved that about him, everything about him on the field," he said. "He always looked like he had fun."

Carr has a lot of Favre in him in the way he can sling the ball all over from different angles. He has become friends with Steve Mariucci, who was Favre's quarterbacks coach for his first four seasons in Green Bay after he was traded from Atlanta. "He knows I love Favre," he said. "He texts me and tells me stories all the time. It was hilarious. Some of the stuff Brett would do just cracks me up."

Rodger was the general sales manager at the dealership. Sheryl was a teacher. They had no intention of packing up their lives and moving to Houston until David insisted.

"Dad, give your two weeks' notice. You guys are all coming," David said.

"David, don't worry about us. We both love our jobs. It's what we do," Rodger said.

David would not take no for an answer. He had told his father when he was drafted that he would never have to work another day in his life.

"You've done enough," David said. "You helped me get here."

So the Carrs sold the house in Bakersfield and moved to Houston. David had a business manager based in California, and his father became his personal assistant in Texas. If he had a card show signing, his father would take him. When it was time to wrap up, it was Rodger who played the bad guy and said his son was done. When David and Melody needed a night out, Rodger and Sheryl came over to take care of Austin. "We kept pretty busy when David first got down there," Rodger said. "We were there to support and take care of everything."

Rodger knew he would have missed being at the games if he'd remained in California. Now, rather than traveling all the time to Houston or watching on the Sunday Ticket on DirecTV, he was right there in Houston starting a new life as his son tried to establish himself as an NFL quarterback. Things went well at first. The family would get together weekly at a restaurant for Friday night dinner and Carr earned the starting job to open his rookie season. The Texans became just the second expansion team to win their opening game when they upset the in-state rival Dallas Cowboys in Houston. Unfortunately for the Carrs, that was the highlight of the season. Casserly had failed to put together an offensive line to protect Carr, and he was sacked an NFL-record seventy-six times. Incredibly, he was able to start all sixteen games. Houston finished 4-12, not unexpected for an expansion team. In Carr's five years with the Texans, they didn't draft an offensive lineman in the first or second round.

Carr, however, was the real casualty. He never recovered from the beating.

At the time, it was the best thing for the family to stick together. David was getting beaten up so badly he needed the moral support. Derek had never been to an NFL game before he saw his brother play. The Texans training facility at the stadium became Derek's second home. He knew every key code and had free run of the place. He would walk in, the receptionist would tell him where his big brother was, and Derek would go find him.

"Do you know the codes?" he was asked.

"Got it," Derek said.

"He's in the weight room," he was told.

Off to the weight room Derek would go.

Derek had tremendous skill in throwing the football. Before David's rookie season started, he was over at his parents' house and took Derek into the backyard to have a catch. They were 50 yards apart. David would throw it to Derek and the little guy would fire it right back. Derek was just in the sixth grade.

"Dad, that kid is not normal," David said.

David lived only a couple of miles from his parents. When it was time for Derek to go to high school, he went to Clements High School in Sugar Land, Texas. The school is named after former Texas governor Bill Clements. It was not known as a real football powerhouse like Hightower or Marshall or Katy. "We didn't know that when we moved there," Rodger said. "Dave got a house and we got a house. That's the school he went to."

David learned the fundamentals of throwing the football from his father, who studied tapes of John Elway and Dan Marino. "He taught himself the mechanics of how to throw a football, and it's still the same stuff we use today," Derek said. "He said, 'Hey, look, Dan Marino gets the ball out quick. John Elway gets the ball out quick.' That's how he taught us. David would teach us the mental side of the game."

David attended Derek's high school games. So would Texans receiver Andre Johnson. David and Derek would watch tape before the games and go over coverages and where to go with the ball.

"The most film we would watch was the Houston film," Derek said. "I would watch it with him and go play my games. I would sit there together with him and say he was playing the Jaguars. David would say, 'Okay, you're going to be the quarterback in this game. Tell me the coverage, tell me where the blitz is coming from, and I'll tell you the routes and you tell me where you're throwing the ball.'"

They would sit for ninety minutes. Derek would make his decision on the blocking assignments he would need to call at the line of scrimmage based on what he saw from the defense, read if a blitz was coming, and find his receiver.

"Okay," David said. "That's one concussion because you didn't get the right guard blocked and you threw a pick."

By the end of the simulated game, Derek was 6 for 38, was sacked twelve times, and had three concussions. But at least it was all in a meeting room with his brother, and it was not unlike playing a video game. And when Derek was playing in his high school games, the game slowed down for him.

Not so for David. Each Sunday he would go out there and get the crap kicked out of him. The Texans couldn't block for him, which naturally made him gun-shy and impacted his decision making. No quarterback, whether it's Tom Brady or Peyton Manning or Brett Favre or Aaron Rodgers—none of them likes to get hit. Now think about a rookie quarterback getting sacked seventy-six times with no experience or history of success in the NFL to rely on and lacking the confidence to believe it would get better.

"It was hard to watch," Derek said. "In college, David would never get hit. The line was protecting him. He would score touchdowns left and right. Then when he got to Houston, he would get hit every play."

The entire Carr family sat and watched those games in the stands in Houston. It was painful. Derek knew that he wanted to play high school football and then college and hopefully make it into the NFL. Watching David play opened his eyes.

"I had to grow up fast and learn. Man, surely the quarterback is not supposed to get hit this much," he said. "Something inside of me said, 'This isn't right.' I honestly didn't know what I was talking about yet. Now that I do know, going back and watching, it's really hard for me. Obviously, I'm his brother, and people take my word for what it's worth because I'm his brother, but he is still to this day the most talented, gifted passer I've ever seen in my life. He went in the first round, first pick, for a reason. It just blows my mind to have a great offensive line with the Raiders. He had the polar opposite. It just hurts my heart."

David was a big believer in his little brother even before he had his breakout season in 2016. "He understands the game more than I did, so his confidence level is off the charts," he said on 95.7 radio in San Francisco. "His leadership ability is kind of where I was never at early on in my career. He's able to go out and get guys that are seven, eight years older than him to actually buy into what he's doing and believe that he can play and believe that he can go out and lead the team."

Derek played on the freshman team at Clements, then an injury elevated him to the starting job on the varsity as a sophomore. By the time Derek was a junior at Clements, when he threw for 1,622 yards and sixteen touchdowns, it was clear he was good enough to play college football. His team was undefeated when they faced Stratford in an early-round game of the Texas 5A State Playoffs. Stratford was also undefeated. They had a senior quarterback named Andrew Luck. Rodger Carr had heard about Luck. He was the best high school quarterback in Texas.

"Derek went off and Andrew went off. Both of them had terrific games," Rodger said. "We ended up winning."

After the game, the quarterbacks met at midfield.

"Man, you're not bad," Luck said.

"You're not bad either," Carr said.

It was the game when everybody realized David's little brother was a very good player. Clements would lose to eventual champion Katy in the quarterfinals.

Luck had already committed to play at Stanford. The next year, Carr would commit to following his brother and play at Fresno State. Stanford and Fresno State, although both in Northern California, have not faced each other in football since 1928. The next time Luck and Carr played against each other was the day before Christmas 2016, nine years after their play-off battle. Sadly, that was the day Carr broke his leg. It's not often that quarterbacks who are matched up in a high school play-off game later face each other in the NFL.

As Derek's star was rising, David's was rapidly falling.

His sack total dropped to just fifteen in his second season, but he was able to start only twelve games. His sack totals in his next three seasons were 49, 68, and 41, but he was able to start every game each season. By the end of Carr's fifth season in Houston, he was released. He was never able to get the Texans close to the play-offs. His best year was his third season when they won seven games, but they then were able to win a total of just eight in his last two years. Casserly was let go by Houston before the 2006 season, and one year later, new general manager Rick Smith cut Carr, who then signed with the Carolina Panthers. He wound up playing twelve years in the NFL but started only four more games, although he did win a Super Bowl XLVI ring as Eli Manning's backup with the Giants.

After Derek Carr's junior year at Clements, there was no reason for the family to remain in Houston other than to allow Derek to finish out high school. David and his family were in Charlotte. Sheryl's father had been diagnosed with brain cancer and the family wanted to return to California. Her father had been the pastor for forty years at the church the Carrs attended. There was a sense of urgency for Derek to get home to be around his grandfather for whatever time he had left, but he was also entrenched as his team's starting quarterback with college scholarship opportunities pouring in.

"Your junior and senior years are the biggest years for you," Derek said. "I remember getting recruited like crazy. Texas high school is something out of this world. I still can't describe it to my friends. There were twenty colleges out in the stands watching your practice."

Derek was torn. He felt an obligation to his team. They were coming off two great seasons. He felt a sense of responsibility to his family.

Rodger went and had a talk with Derek.

"Son, the decision is yours to make. If you want to stay, we will absolutely stay. If you want to go back to California, we are going to sell this house and get a house there and we'll be gone. I want you to know we are going to support whatever you want to do and there will never be a discussion beyond that," Rodger said.

That was a lot of responsibility to put on a high school kid.

"Hey, Dad, I want to go home. I want to go back to Bakersfield and play in front of Poppa and the family and friends," Derek said.

"Seriously?" Rodger said.

The hardest part for Derek was leaving his friends. "There would only be eight returning guys on the varsity," Derek said. "So when I left they only had seven guys returning on an eighty-five-man team. That was hard for me. 'Man, am I really leaving them out to dry? Hope they're not mad at me. Hope they will still be my friends for life.' At the same time, the only grandfather I've ever known in life was sick. I loved him so much. We were trying to get home for that. I wanted to spend time with him. It was just the right time to go back just to be together with all our family again. It was tough on everybody. Man, I just felt so grateful. My dad always treated me like a grown man."

Carr's friends understood. Family over football. "But like any high school kid, you don't want to leave your buddies that you used to hang out with for the last six or seven years," Derek said. "What was really cool about that is they stuck behind me. Some of them come to games now. When we played in Denver in 2015, we got to hang out after the game. The night before the game I got to see them for a couple of minutes. We all stayed close. Looking back on it, it was the right decision."

It was up to Rodger to find a high school where Derek could walk in as the unquestioned starter at quarterback for his senior year. As terrific a player as Derek had become, it wasn't going to be easy finding the right situation. He was being heavily recruited and needed to stay on the field.

David and Darren played at Stockdale High School. David even has his name on the scoreboard. Stockdale was in the midst of a coaching change, and Rodger didn't think that would be good for Derek. Rodger called the offensive coordinator at Stockdale, who had also been there when David played. He was going to remain at the school as long as they didn't hire this one candidate who wanted to implement the wing-T and just run the ball.

"I don't want to throw the ball three times a game my senior year," Derek said.

They hired the coach. Stockdale was off the list.

"Oh, wow, what do we do?" Rodger said.

A friend of his called. "Rodger, where are you sending Derek?" he asked.

"I'm not sure right now," he said.

"Bakersfield Christian High School, they just won the league and the Valley," his friend said.

"If they just won the league and the Valley, they must have a pretty good quarterback," Rodger said.

"Yeah, they do. His name is Jake Peterson, but he played wide receiver as a sophomore and just played quarterback because they needed a quarterback," he said.

Rodger called the head coach and told him Derek wanted to play for him but didn't want him to push Peterson aside. He was told Peterson was six foot four and wanted to go back to wide receiver. The coach wanted Derek, Rodger and Derek wanted Bakersfield Christian, and the match was made. The team was 12-1 with Carr and won a sectional championship. Carr wanted to go where he could throw the ball. In his senior year, he tossed forty-six touchdowns and threw for 4,067 yards.

"To this day, Derek actually trains with Jake Peterson in the off-season when he's not in camp," Rodger said. "Jake is up in the Bay Area and has his own training facility. So Derek goes to him. It's pretty cool."

The only negative: Carr's grandfather passed away prior to the season and didn't get to see him play.

His college choices came down to Fresno State, Utah, and SMU.

Derek chose Fresno State and had an outstanding college career. After throwing just 10 passes as a freshman and then redshirting his second season, he was a three-year starter with a 28-15 record with 12,843 yards passing, 113 touchdowns, and 24 interceptions.

Twelve years after he accompanied his big brother to the NFL draft, Derek was projected to be a first-round pick. Not the first overall pick, but at least in the first round. It was a long first day. He didn't get selected in the first round, but three quarterbacks did: Blake Bortles went third to the Jaguars, Johnny Manziel went twenty-second to the Browns, and Teddy Bridgewater was the last pick of the first round by the Vikings at number 32.

Carr was the fourth overall pick in the second round by the Raiders, who had selected linebacker Khalil Mack in the first round. If the Raiders get to the Super Bowl in the prime years of the careers of Carr and Mack, it will be remembered as one of the best drafts of all time. Even if Carr was thrilled to be picked by the Raiders, who play so close to where he grew up, he was disappointed he was not selected in the first round.

He had two things working against him: He did not play at a football powerhouse; and, perhaps even more important, his brother David did not live up to expectations.

"If a team ever looks at it that way, I don't even want to play for them because they are looking at the glass half empty all the time," Derek said. "I would rather have somebody look at it the way I look at it: What an experience I got, to have a brother who played in the NFL for twelve years, who went through all the highs and went through all the lowest of lows and he learned from it and grew from it. Now turn the tape on and say this is what he looks like now. Just judge me off that. That's the team I want to play for."

The Carrs gathered at David's house for the 2014 draft. Derek felt he had experienced the draft in New York with his brother and wanted to just be with family now that it was his turn. "Derek wanted to go in the first round so badly," Rodger said. "He wanted to be like his brother. As the first-round picks went by that day, I would see Derek's face changing a little bit. He was getting mad."

David last played in the NFL in 2012 in his second stint with the Giants as Eli Manning's backup. He announced his retirement the next summer. There was some talk before Derek's draft in 2014 that some teams were interested in bringing David in as a backup and veteran mentor for his brother.

"The main reason they like it is because you're going to get a vet who wants to help the rookie, while at the same time he is going to push harder than anybody because he wants the best for me," Derek said on 95.7 in San Francisco a few weeks before the draft. "There's no division in that locker room because we're both rooting for each other. We're not saying one thing behind each other's back."

The family dispersed after the first round and reconvened the next evening for round two. Several teams had told Derek

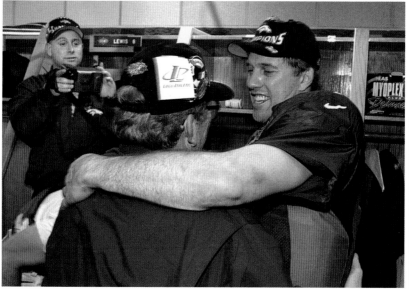

The emotion was off the charts in the Broncos locker room in San Diego following Super Bowl XXXII. The Broncos, underdogs to the Packers, had just pulled off the upset for John Elway's first championship after he lost his first three Super Bowls by a combined score of 136–40. Moments after Denver owner Pat Bowlen held up the trophy and proclaimed, "This one's for John," Elway was in the locker room hugging his father, Jack.

John Elway shakes the hand of his father and best friend Jack Elway after beating the Falcons in Super Bowl XXXIII in Miami. It was Elway's second consecutive championship. It also turned out to be the final game of his legendary career. Three months after the game, he announced his retirement, which allowed him to walk away a champion as he neared his fortieth birthday.

Jim Harbaugh and the University of Michigan were a perfect match when the former coach of the 49ers was hired by his alma mater in 2015. Harbaugh's father, Jack, was a former Wolverines assistant coach under Bo Schembechler, and little Jim once walked into Bo's office and sat behind Bo's desk. It wasn't long before Harbaugh had Michigan back in contention for the national title.

It was a lot less stressful when Jim (left), Jack (middle), and John (right) Harbaugh got together for a coaches clinic in Ann Arbor than when it was Jim versus John in Super Bowl XLVII, dubbed the HarBowl, in New Orleans. Jim's 49ers put on a great rally and nearly pulled off the comeback against John's Ravens, but Jack and his wife, Jackie, knew that no matter what, one of their sons would be euphoric and the other would be miserable. After Jim's first season back at Michigan, his parents moved around the corner from him in Ann Arbor.

They literally loaded up the Carr and all moved to Houston in 2002. With older sons David, the number-one pick of the Houston Texans, and Darren, playing at the University of Houston, Rodger and Sheryl Carr decided to move with young son Derek to Houston so the family could stay together. It worked out well for Derek, who established himself as a terrific high school quarterback at Clements—he beat Andrew Luck in a play-off game—before moving back to California for his senior year.

Football was always a big thing in the Carr house. Now with Derek (left) the only Carr still on the road, Darren (second from left) is running a training center with help from David (second from right) and the patriarch, Rodger (far right); the family is back together. But that will change in 2019 when the Raiders are scheduled to move to Las Vegas.

There's nothing like having big brothers. Derek (the little guy) is all dressed up to hang out with Darren (middle) and David (right). Now that David is done playing football, he works for the NFL Network. Before Derek was drafted in 2014, there was talk that David would sign with whichever team picked Derek and be his backup/mentor. This picture would certainly have gotten a lot of laughs in the locker room.

Ryan Fitzpatrick took thousands of snaps in his football career, but there always has to be a first. And this was it. He's lined up behind his father, Mike, with older identical twin brothers Jason and Brandon getting ready to play some defense against the future NFL quarterback.

Ryan Fitzpatrick is a smart guy. He went to Harvard. His father, Mike, would often take a redeye flight on Friday night from Phoenix to Boston to see Ryan play at Harvard Stadium. Just because Harvard is known more for producing presidents than quarterbacks, Fitz's goal was always to make it to the NFL.

Joe Flacco was a big-time football and baseball player in high school. Although his high school helmet looks like it's from the University of Michigan, his best college offer was from Pitt. That didn't work out and he transferred and played two seasons at Delaware.

Joe Flacco has always had a strong support system with his parents, Karen and Steve. Joe is the oldest of the five Flacco kids, and here he is at Audubon High School in New Jersey with his brother Mike, who is two years younger.

Joe Flacco took a circuitous route to the NFL after playing at a small New Jersey high school, Pitt, and Delaware, but in 2008 the Baltimore Ravens made him the eighteenth pick in the first round. The Flacco family then drove the 115 miles from Audubon, New Jersey, to the Ravens offices in Owings Mills, Maryland, for his introductory press conference.

The Brothers Manning are very close. Cooper (second from left) and Peyton (second from right) are Eli's biggest fans, along with their parents, Archie and Olivia. Cooper had a promising career as a wide receiver cut short before his freshman season at Ole Miss when he was diagnosed with a career-ending neck injury. He is a very successful businessman in New Orleans and has lived out his football dreams through the careers of his brothers.

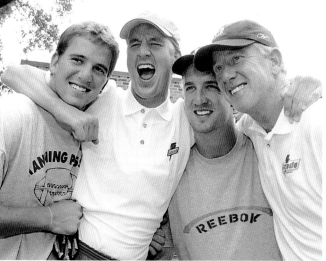

Archie had the ball but Eli (far left) and Cooper wanted it as Peyton looked on in the yard of their home in the Garden District in New Orleans. Archie was the quarterback for his boys' favorite game: "Amazing Catches." Archie would throw the ball just far enough for his sons to dive for it. If that catch wasn't amazing enough, Archie would throw it a little farther.

Christopher Simms, already showing he's a left-hander with his ice pop, visits his dad, Phil, at New York Giants training camp in 1983 in Pleasantville, New York. Simms was in his fifth year with the Giants and Chris was almost three years old. Twenty years later, Chris Simms was rookie quarterback in training camp with the Tampa Bay Buccaneers.

Chris Simms was wearing his father's familiar number 11 in the colors that resembled the rival Dallas Cowboys as a quarterback in the seventh grade. Phil didn't get to see Chris play very often in middle school, high school, college, or the NFL. Phil was usually out of town preparing to broadcast a football game.

Chris Simms (left) was in his fourth year with the Tampa B Bucs when they played a gam 2006 at Giants Stadium again his father's former team. Chri was not active for the game, b he did receive a pregame visi from his younger brother, Ma who was then a senior playin quarterback at Don Bosco Pre New Jersey. Matt went on to p in the NFL as well.

Even at a young age, Jameis Winston looked the part of a future NFL quarterback. He was a two-sport star in baseball and football in high school and college and could have made it as a hard-throwing right-handed starting pitcher. It's hard to argue with his decision: He was the first overall pick in the 2015 draft by the Tampa Bay Bucs.

Jameis Winston chose to spend draft day back home in Alabama in 2015 with family and friends even though it was known he would be the first overall pick. When the Bucs introduced him at a press conference the next day at team headquarters in Tampa, he was joined by his father Antonor, little brother Jonah, mother Loretta, and sister Ayuna.

Nick Montana, Joe's younger son, had his choice of some of the top football programs in the country. He was considered one of the best high school quarterback prospects. He chose the University of Washington. After redshirting as a freshman and then getting beaten out for the starting job the next season, he transferred after one year on the varsity and played one year at a junior college and then two years at Tulane.

Joe Montana's legacy at Notre Dame included winning the 1977 National Championship when he took over as the starting quarterback in the fourth game of the season and didn't lose the rest of the way.

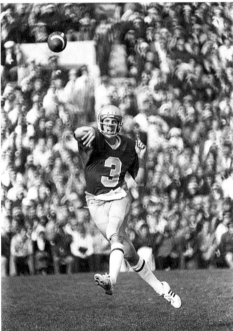

Like father, like son? Nate Montana's jump pass brought back fond memories of his dad's days at Notre Dame, even if the results didn't measure up. Joe wore number 3 at Notre Dame but made number 16 famous in his fourteen years with the 49ers. When Nate, the older of the two Montana boys, joined the Fighting Irish as a preferred walk-on quarterback in 2008, coach Charlie Weis added to the pressure by assigning him jersey number 16. Nate's most extended action came in a 2010 game against Michigan when he came off the bench.

prior to the draft that if he was available at their spot in the first round, they were going to take him. Then he was available and they selected another player. "That was my first taste of how much of a business this is," he said. "I knew it. I had seen it. I had seen it with my brother. He had told me and told me. But I had finally experienced it for myself. It gave me a different perspective."

The predraft rumors indicated the Browns were going to take Carr with the first of their first-round picks. But when they traded down to the eighth spot, they selected cornerback Justin Gilbert. They still owned the twenty-second pick and Carr was still on the board. "I'm not kidding you, when they were on the clock, I was sitting there going, 'Here we go. We're going to Cleveland,'" Derek said "And then they didn't pick me and I thought, 'Man, this night is getting crazy.'"

Who did the Browns select? Texas A&M quarterback Johnny Manziel. That was a mistake. Manziel became a trainwreck off the field. In the few times he was on the field, he showed no traits of ever becoming a franchise quarterback. He was out of Cleveland after just two seasons. The Browns would love to get a do-over on that one.

When Rodger walked back into David's house for the start of round two, Derek told his father that "God had slapped me in the face. 'You want what you want or what I want?'"

He had relied on his faith to get him over his disappointment. He was thrilled when the Raiders picked him. The front office embraced the experience he had being around his brother with the Texans and felt it would be beneficial to his career. "I really wanted a team to look at it that way rather than say, 'Oh man, they only won four games every year or they only won seven games or didn't win the Super Bowl or win the division, so I guess he's not going to do it,'" Derek said. "I don't want to play for people like that."

When Rodger met Reggie McKenzie, he thanked him for keeping his son in California. "I know that he saw what David went through and what the family went through," he said. "He goes, 'Rodger, one thing I will promise you is that Derek will always have protection. I will always give him protection.' So I thought that was really cool. I'm grateful. He said it and now he's doing it."

In his first three seasons, Carr was sacked a total of seventy-one times, five fewer than his brother was sacked in his rookie season alone. Derek Carr established himself as one of the best young quarterbacks in the NFL with a bright future ahead for himself and his team. The Raiders had been a burial ground for coaches and quarterbacks for more than a decade, but Carr changed the culture of the organization. "I wanted to go somewhere I was wanted. I wanted to go somewhere they loved me and believed in who I was and how I lead and how I play the game," he said. "I was completely happy to be picked by Oakland because that is where I wanted to go. But I was hoping it was at number 5 and not number 36."

The Texans had the first overall pick in the first round and the first pick in the second round and passed on Carr twice. The first time was understandable. They selected pass rusher Jadeveon Clowney. In the second round, with the thirty-third overall selection, they took Xavier Su'a-Filo, who became a full-time starter by the middle of his second season. Even so, he's a guard. The Texans didn't have any contact with Carr before the draft, obviously scared off by bringing another Carr to the franchise after their experience with David. Too bad for them, but this Carr would have been perfect for them. As Carr was becoming a star, the Texans were still looking for a quarterback. Before the 2016 season, they signed Broncos free agent quarterback Brock Osweiler to a four-year $72 million contract that included $37 million in guaranteed money. One year later, they traded him. They would have been much better off spending their money on the latest-model Carr.

"I would have loved to play for [Texans owner] Mr. [Bob] McNair, and I say that just with respect," Carr said. "I'm just trying to give a compliment to Mr. McNair. I love him. The city was great to myself and my family. We have nothing but respect for that city and I have nothing but respect for Mr. McNair."

Rodger now helps run the Carr Elite Football Clinic in Bakersfield. They train fifty kids per week from eight years old up to college age. "I'm a football freak," Rodger said.

Rodger added to his football knowledge watching Fresno State practices, along with what David has taught him and what Derek passes down. If Derek had not been injured so late in the 2016 season, perhaps the Raiders would have made it to Super Bowl LI. The game was in Houston, where the Carr football journey really started for Derek and his father. Instead, it's where the Raiders' season ended. From now on, they need to avoid Houston.

RYAN FITZPATRICK
The Harvard Man

Mike Fitzpatrick pulled his car up in front of his son Ryan's dorm at Harvard University to begin the process of moving him in for his freshman year at the finest college in the country.

Many universities with big-time football programs will house the freshmen athletes together, giving them a chance to bond, or place them in a location that makes it easier to get to practice every day. Harvard was different. Football players roomed with government majors who roomed with computer science students who roomed with premed students who roomed with future presidents.

One big, happy, very smart family.

It didn't take long for Ryan Fitzpatrick, from Gilbert, Arizona, to understand that Harvard was a unique kind of place. He had lived with the football players for two weeks of summer training camp before moving into his assigned dormitory for the school year. He had been assigned to Grays, a dorm in

Elm Yard, part of the famed Harvard Yard. It was a four-story building constructed in 1863.

His parents had come out to meet him once he was able to move into Grays.

As the Fitzpatricks unloaded his belongings and all things necessary to survive freshman year, a large van parked right behind them. It was the fall of 2001. Ryan immediately noticed Secret Service agents surrounding the van.

"What the heck is going on?" he said.

Ten months earlier, Al Gore, the vice president, had lost to George W. Bush in the most controversial presidential election in United States history, complete with hanging chads. Now the door of the van opened and Al and Tipper Gore and their freshman son, Albert Gore III, emerged.

Mike turned to Ryan and whispered, "We ain't in Kansas anymore."

Gore III walked onto the football team as a lineman. "He was on the team at least for one year," Ryan said. "He wasn't on the team very long."

Ryan Fitzpatrick's high school was 99 percent white and 85 percent Mormon (his family is not) and 0 percent children of a former vice president.

"You're just thrown in with everybody else," he said. "So that was one of the coolest parts for me. One of my roommates was from Newport Beach in California, but he had been going to a boarding school since he was eight. Another was from Madison, New Jersey, and he talked funny and had a big nose.

There was another kid that was Indian. I grew up where everybody was the same. Then I went to Harvard and I said, 'Oh my gosh. This is what the world is like. Holy crap.' It was an eye-opening experience for me."

The Ivy League produces a lot of politicians, lawyers, doctors, even dropouts who invent Facebook and just eggheads who go on to become the stars of whatever field they choose. NFL quarterbacks and other players? Well, not so much. Harvard has turned out eight presidents of the United States, but Fitzpatrick is its only quarterback.

It may not rival the Big 10 or the SEC, but that's because student athletes who decide to attend Ivy League schools don't often have realistic expectations of making it in professional football. They want to save the world and make money in other ways.

Ryan Fitzpatrick was smart enough to get into Harvard based on his grades, but in a way he was disappointed to be going there because he believed he was better than an Ivy League player. Colorado and Colorado State liked him but would make an offer only if they couldn't get quarterbacks higher on their list. His first choice was Arizona State, where his parents went to college, but they were not interested. Not even being a big Jake Plummer fan was enough to get him a scholarship.

"I wanted to play at ASU. I wanted to play at Stanford or Duke or Notre Dame and nobody came knocking, so that's why I turned elsewhere," he said. "My one scholarship offer was from Eastern Washington."

He liked Timm Rosenbach, the offensive coordinator and former NFL quarterback. Eastern Washington was in the Big Sky Conference, which is hardly made up of football powerhouses. Fitzpatrick planned five college visits and told his father he wanted to see Princeton from the Ivy League. Mike grew up in New Jersey before going to ASU and making a life in Arizona. Ryan at least wanted to take the opportunity to see where his father spent his early years, so he accepted the invitation and asked his father to make the trip with him.

"We flew out to Princeton," Mike said. "That is what I thought the extent of it would be."

Word traveled fast from Princeton up to Cambridge, Massachusetts. One day after returning home, Fitzpatrick received a call from Harvard: We'll be out to your home to see you tomorrow. "You go to the best school in the country, you're a Harvard man," was the hard sell.

The Harvard men left the house. Fitzpatrick turned to his father. "I want to go to Harvard," he said.

Mike pushed academics as hard as he pushed athletics with his four sons. But he felt if Ryan picked Harvard, he was conceding that he would never play in the NFL.

"Ryan, you realize that you have given up here anything beyond college. Nobody knows anything about Harvard football," Mike said.

"Dad, if I'm good enough, they will find me," Ryan said.

Mike Fitzpatrick was blown away by his son's positive attitude. "To me, that was the most incredible thing to ever come out of a seventeen-year-old's mouth," he said.

Fitzpatrick had the credentials to get into Harvard. His parents created an atmosphere in the house that success in the classroom was not negotiable. Ryan held up his end of the deal. He had Harvard-quality grades. He was sixth in his graduating class of 750. That put him in the top 1 percent. He had one or two Bs in four years, but the rest were straight As. He was off the charts on the standardized tests, although Fitzpatrick was not interested in revealing his SAT score.

"It was high enough to get into Harvard," he said.

What was it?

"It was good enough to get into Harvard," he said.

Can you provide a number?

"Nah," he said.

Did you get a perfect 1600?

"I did not," he said.

Close?

"I'm not telling you," he said.

Mike Fitzpatrick was more than happy to reveal Ryan's SAT score: 1580. He had a perfect 800 on the math and a near-perfect 780 on the English. Pretty impressive, but what happened with the couple of questions he missed? "English wasn't our thing in our house," Mike said. "We were definitely more math and science."

Just to prove he didn't use up all his brainpower at Harvard, he scored 48 out of 50 on the Wonderlic intelligence test given by the NFL to draft prospects at the Scouting Combine. He completed the test in just nine minutes out of the allotted twelve. He left one question blank, meaning of the questions he answered, he got forty-eight correct and just one wrong. He tied for the third-highest score ever among NFL draft prospects and tied Alabama's Greg McElroy for the best score ever by a quarterback. Punter–wide receiver Pat McInally, another Harvard man, is the only player tested by the NFL to score a perfect 50.

That helped convince NFL teams, if they needed to be convinced, that processing the playbook was not going to be an issue for Fitzpatrick. Deep sideline passes were another story. If he had the quarterback skills to match his mental skills, he would have been the first pick in the draft. Comparing him intellectually to other players was not fair. Comparing his quarterback skills, as well as his experience against superior competition, to the top quarterbacks in the draft was not fair, either.

Fitzpatrick believes football helped get him into Harvard. "When you sit there and you look at the statistics of who doesn't get into Harvard, it's unbelievable," he said. "They say they accept fifteen hundred kids per year. But look at how many applicants there are—I think to say, 'Yeah, I would have got in no matter what...'; it's very difficult to get in without any sort of help, so football definitely helped me."

According to the *Harvard Crimson* student newspaper, Harvard received 34,295 applications for the class of 2018. It accepted 2,023 students, which is an acceptance rate of just 5.9 percent. "They do the band system," Fitzpatrick said. "So there's four different bands, and depending on your test score and the type of player you are, they use your GPA and your SAT or ACT and that puts you in band one, two, three, or four."

The football program was allowed to accept an unlimited number of players from the top band. There was a decreasing limit on each of the other bands. "I was a top-band guy, so they didn't have to go out of their way to say, 'Hey, let's get this guy in,'" Fitzpatrick said. "But to say that I would have gotten in on my own merit without football—that would have been tough."

It's not easy to maintain grades at an Ivy League school and still put in all the time required for football. Ivy League schools do not provide athletic scholarships, so the players on the team are serious about football. They are not just showing up to maintain their scholarships.

"The academic demands are ridiculous," Mike Fitzpatrick said. "I went to ASU. I can't imagine what Harvard is like. We didn't groom him for Harvard. We were from the West Coast. Harvard was never in our plans. We didn't check all the boxes in getting him ready to go there. He went to a public school in Arizona. He didn't go to any kind of a specialty school. The whole deal was pretty good. It was unbelievable."

Fitzpatrick's dream of playing big-time college football was not going to happen. Mike told his son to decide where he wanted to go to school and they would figure out how to pay for it. "That's one of the best things he told me leading up to college," Ryan said. "My father told me, 'Look, you can pick any school in the country. I don't care if we've got to pay for it or we need to ask for help or you get a scholarship. You make the decision on where you want to go.'"

Fitzpatrick didn't realize at first what a financial burden it would be for him to attend a private institution and not be on a football scholarship, especially with his twin brothers, who are eighteen months older than him, already in college—Jason was a breaststroke swimmer at Notre Dame, and Brandon was a high school quarterback but didn't play at Northern Arizona. The youngest brother, Shaun, four years younger than Ryan, would go on to play tight end at Northern Arizona.

Ryan received some financial aid from Harvard, but his dad reassured him that "he was going to be there for me all the time and provide me with unlimited resources to do what I wanted to, whether it was football or anything else."

He wanted to go to ASU. Harvard was the best he could do.

"To not even get a sniff from Arizona State was really tough for me," he said. "But a consolation prize of, 'Oh, I'm going to Harvard,' ended up working out okay."

Fitzpatrick was an economics major and likely would have pursued a job on Wall Street if he hadn't made it in the NFL, but that's not how he approached his time at Harvard. He wanted to soak up all the knowledge he could and take advantage of all the university had to offer, but there was no doubt football was very important to him. Even though no quarterback from Harvard had ever started a game in the NFL, there was at least a history of success—although the list was short—of Ivy Leaguers who had gone on to have productive careers in pro football.

Sid Luckman, who played at Columbia and then for the Chicago Bears, is in the Pro Football Hall of Fame. In 2016, Fitzpatrick broke Luckman's record for most touchdown passes by an Ivy League quarterback in the NFL. Chuck Bednarik, a hard-hitting linebacker and dominant center from Penn, also made the Hall of Fame after an outstanding career with the

Philadelphia Eagles. He was the first overall pick in the 1949 draft. When talking about vicious tacklers in NFL history, Bednarik goes right to the top of the list.

In a 1960 game against the New York Giants, his right shoulder caught Frank Gifford squarely under the chin and Gifford went down in a heap. He was knocked out. Many of the Giants thought it was a cheap shot, and Gifford, who was the golden boy of the NFL, was taken to the hospital. He sat out the 1961 season before returning. The picture of Bednarik standing over the fallen Gifford is iconic.

The list of successful Ivy League players includes running back Calvin Hill and safety Gary Fencik from Yale; running back Ed Marinaro, a runner-up for the Heisman Trophy in 1971 from Cornell; quarterback Jay Fiedler from Dartmouth; and quarterback Jason Garrett from Princeton. They had careers of varying degrees of success in the NFL.

More than two dozen players from Harvard made it into the NFL, including McInally, center Matt Birk, and offensive lineman Dan Jiggetts.

"I played a little bit freshman and sophomore year, but there was a locked-in guy who started my freshman year. He came back for a fifth year and got an added year of eligibility my sophomore year, so he was the starter," Fitzpatrick said. "I ended up starting some games that year, so by junior and senior year, I was the guy."

He never took football for granted. It may not have been Alabama or Michigan, but it was not an intramural or club sport, either. If he played well, Fitzpatrick was right, the NFL scouts would notice. He was serious about trying to make it his career. "Football was very important to me," Ryan said. "It was never, 'Okay, I'm here and I'm doing football for fun.'"

But this was not Florida State or Ohio State or some football factory where the players' times for the 40-yard dash are more important than the GPA. This was Harvard. Football counts. Academics count more.

"It was tough because football is serious business," Fitzpatrick said. "We're all college athletes trying to be as good a player as we can. Because of the expectations in the way it was set up by people who were there before me, you go to class, you get your work done, you also do all your football stuff. Expectations are high, but there is a great example set by people there before you."

He would stay up late at night like the rest of the Harvard students finishing a paper or cramming for an exam. "You certainly learn right away how to manage your time and make the best use of your time," he said. "There are plenty of things put on you being a student at Harvard."

If there were academic conflicts in the spring, academics came first. But players didn't miss practice in the fall. The hardest class Fitzpatrick faced in four years was upper-level economics, which has surely helped him understand the business of the NFL as he bounced around from one team to the next in his NFL career until the total reached seven in his first thirteen seasons. He appreciates his Harvard degree. "It's awesome," he said. "It's unbelievable. Look at the list of people who have gone there. There is a rich history."

II

Ryan Fitzpatrick was an accomplished swimmer and triathlete before he even got to high school. He played baseball and soccer, and his father was involved in everything. Mike Fitzpatrick was hands-on with the decisions of what sports all four of his boys would play until loosening the grip when they reached high school.

He thought it was critical for his kids to play individual sports and not limit themselves to team sports. That's why Ryan was not permitted to play on a travel baseball team and play year-round even though he was an excellent player. "That's the type of thing we never let happen," Mike said. "No, you're going to play a mix of other things."

Off the diamond and into the pool. "They didn't really have a choice whether they swam or not," he said. "That's what I was saying to them. Until you get to high school, I get to pick which sports you play. Then when you get to high school, you get to pick what sports you play. I'll be totally hands-off. You get to do what you want. Obviously, he picked football."

He wanted his children to experience everything before they entered high school so they could make an informed decision concerning what to pursue. "It was pretty orchestrated," Mike said. "It was not with the thought in mind of ever having the NFL in the future. I just wanted to always set them up for high school, so they would have a good experience playing high school sports. It was important they did a lot of things instead of specializing. The tendency...even when they were growing up, was to specialize. Ryan was a really good baseball player. He was a catcher. During the Little League years, he was a dominant baseball player in our town."

Not quite as good a catcher as Tom Brady, who was taken by the Montreal Expos in the eighteenth round of the 1995 draft. "I'm so happy I stuck with football," Brady wrote in a Facebook post in 2016 on the twenty-first anniversary of his being drafted by the Expos.

The Fitzpatrick boys did not present their father with any pushback to his heavy-handed approach. Jason, one of the twins, told his father when he reached high school that he didn't want to play football anymore. His twin, Brandon, was a quarterback and was a better player. Jason wanted to do something else. He concentrated on swimming and ended up competing for Notre Dame.

"It was a very competitive household," Ryan said.

"Certainly, there was an expectation to be different from the other kids, whether it was academically or athletically," Mike said. "Average wasn't acceptable."

From the age of five until he was twelve, Ryan was swimming every weekend in the summer. "Every sport we did, my dad was coaching in it or very involved in it and it was the most important thing in the world at that moment," Ryan said. "Because it was important for him, I think that rubbed off on all of us. It was so important to all of us."

There has be something different about the atmosphere in a home that produces a student who goes to Harvard who is also an athlete good enough to make it as a professional quarterback.

"He just loved being involved in our lives, especially in the sporting aspect of it," Ryan said. "He always pushed us academically. The standard was you had to be the best at everything you do. We tried to be the best at every single thing we did."

Fitzpatrick produced almost completely straight As through each level of school. He was amazed that his father, who worked nine-to-five jobs, would manage to make it over in time for all his practices just about every day from the time he was four straight through high school. He would stand to the side at football practice. He didn't interfere with the coaches.

When the football scholarship offers did not come rolling in as Fitzpatrick hoped, he never sat down to have a heart-to-heart with his father to discuss his frustration. They did not have that kind of relationship. His father had only insisted that he outwork everybody and good things would happen. "He's kind of an old-school dad," Ryan said. "When he was upset with me, it was more silent treatment than it was yelling at me. He was always there for me, but it wasn't like we sat down at dinner every night and talked about our feelings."

Fitzpatrick's decision to enroll at Harvard presented logistical problems for his father. The youngest, Shaun, was then a freshman playing Friday night high school football in Arizona. Harvard's schedule was limited to games in the Northeast. Mike had been so involved and so supportive for the first eighteen years of Ryan's life that he wasn't about to stop. He came up with a plan to attend Shaun's games and then head straight to the airport for a red-eye flight to Boston to get to Harvard Stadium for Ryan's home games.

The flight would land in Boston at 9 a.m. Harvard's home games were at noon. Even though Ryan was with the team getting prepared for the game, Mike would go to Ryan's dorm room, his roommates would let him in, and he would lie down on Ryan's bed for an hour, take a shower, and then go to the game. He went to every home game. It was impossible to get to the away games at Cornell in Ithaca, New York, or Dartmouth in Hanover, New Hampshire, in time for kickoff. The University of Pennsylvania is in Philadelphia and Columbia University is in New York, so those were not a problem. If there was a nonstop flight from Phoenix, Mike was getting to the game.

"I'd see him standing there disheveled before my games to give me a big hug and say, 'Okay, let's go today,'" Ryan said. "That explains my dad probably better than anything else. That commitment was there from the day I was born until today."

Just his father's presence provided motivation and inspiration. He had come so far, and gone through such an effort to get to the game, how could Ryan not play his best? Friday night football in Gilbert, Arizona, followed by Saturday afternoon football in Cambridge, Massachusetts, is not an easy doubleheader. But he loved the effort his father made to get to the games.

"Yeah, it's awesome," Ryan said. "It's unbelievable, but that sums him up and that probably sums up our relationship. We were the most important thing to him always, and it had nothing to do with, 'Okay, my son is going to the NFL.' It's just, 'I want to be there to support him.'"

Ryan became Harvard's starter as a junior, but not even his father was focused on a potential NFL career. He had sixteen touchdowns and eight interceptions and completed 60 percent of his passes. Again, it was the Ivy League. Wall Street, for sure. The NFL, not really. His advanced economics class was the most difficult he took in his four years at Harvard, but deciphering Bill Belichick's defense without the physical skills of Brady or Peyton Manning made a career in the NFL unlikely.

"Never crossed my mind," Mike said. "He was a pretty good college football player, but I realized he was playing in the Ivy League and I wasn't sure."

Between Fitzpatrick's junior and senior years, Harvard coach Tim Murphy called Mike Fitzpatrick. He told him he was starting to receive calls from a lot of agents who were interested in representing his son. He wanted to direct all the calls to Mike and keep them away from Ryan, so he could concentrate on his academics and the football team.

"Dad, just narrow it down to three and we'll figure it out," Ryan said.

Fitzpatrick still had no idea if he was going to get drafted. He started reading the draft previews in his senior year and kept seeing his name. "Oh my God," he said. "They're talking about me?"

If he indeed had any plans to go to work for a large financial firm, he messed it up his senior year by leading Harvard to a perfect 10-0 season. The Crimson were 7-0 in the Ivy League. Fitzpatrick threw thirteen touchdowns and six interceptions, and completed 57.2 percent of his passes. He played himself into the conversation for the 2005 NFL Draft.

He was invited to the Scouting Combine, aced the Wonderlic

and the interviews, and then had to play the waiting game to find out if and when and where he would be drafted.

The question he was asked repeatedly by coaches, general managers, and personnel directors at the combine: "Do you really want to play football with a degree from Harvard?"

His answer was always the same. "Yes," he said.

His father was not happy with the NFL inquisition. "It was almost like a reverse discrimination thing going on," he said.

The first three rounds were conducted the first day. The 49ers selected Utah quarterback Alex Smith first overall. The biggest surprise was that Cal quarterback Aaron Rodgers, who was in contention with Smith to be San Francisco's choice, dropped all the way down to the Packers' spot at number 24 overall, and they developed him to succeed Brett Favre.

Fitzpatrick had a feeling the Patriots might take him. They had multiple picks in the seventh round and had been looking to secure a young quarterback as a backup to Brady. Not long before the draft, Patriots offensive coordinator Josh McDaniels met Fitzpatrick at Harvard Stadium for a workout. "I felt I had a great workout," Fitzpatrick said. "We had great communication."

The first day of the draft went by and Fitzpatrick's name was not called. That was no surprise. But it was only going to take one team to have a conviction about him and that could happen any time in the final four rounds. He was watching the draft back home in Arizona with his parents and family. He had specifically told his father he did not want any friends over to the house. It would be embarrassing if 255 players were drafted and he was not one of them.

Mike had seen that the scouting services ranked Ryan the fifth-best quarterback prospect on one report and the seventh on another. "I just fell out of my chair," he said. "He didn't really throw the ball that much. He was a running quarterback for the most part in college. He threw some, but he wasn't putting up huge numbers. How the heck did they find him? Then it hit: 'Holy smokes, this is going to happen.'"

Jason Campbell was also a first-round pick, by the Redskins. No quarterbacks were taken in the second round, and then Charlie Frye, Andrew Walter, and David Greene were taken in the third round.

If the scouting services were correct, Fitzpatrick would be the first quarterback off the board on the second day of the draft. Two more quarterbacks went in the fourth round: Kyle Orton and Stefan LeFors. Okay, the fifth round wouldn't be so bad; but only Dan Orlovsky and Adrian McPherson were selected. So far, family and friends were kept to a minimum at the Fitzpatrick house.

"The sixth round, the doorbell starts ringing," Fitzpatrick said.

What would be wrong with the sixth round? Wasn't Brady a sixth-round pick in 2000? By the 2005 draft, he had already won three of his five Super Bowls. Derek Anderson was the only quarterback taken in the sixth round.

Often players will say they would rather be a free agent and in a position to field multiple offers than be drafted in the seventh round as an afterthought. But this is where Fitzpatrick was confident the Patriots would take him. He felt he'd had an impressive workout for McDaniels. They had hit it off. McDaniels's offense was complicated but not too complicated for a Harvard man. It would have been a pretty neat story if the team from Foxborough, the defending Super Bowl champions, drafted a quarterback from their own backyard in Cambridge.

James Kilian from Tulsa became the twelfth quarterback selected when he went to the Chiefs in the seventh round. The Patriots were up one spot later at number 230. There were only twenty-six picks remaining. This was the spot. "Then it rolls across the screen that the New England Patriots select Matt Cassel," Ryan Fitzpatrick said. "I've lived the whole draft process and I have no idea who this guy is. I've never heard of him. How is somebody who isn't even part of the draft process selected over me? Who is this guy?"

Cassel was a backup at Southern Cal. He did not start any games in his four seasons at USC and threw only 33 passes.

I'm definitely not getting drafted, Fitzpatrick thought.

His father had invited a houseful of people. Thirty people were gathered around the television.

"That's exactly what I didn't want," Ryan said. "I didn't want to have to go out there and say, 'Hey, I didn't get drafted.'"

He was in a back room in the house. The phone rang. It was Jason Garrett, the quarterbacks coach of the Miami Dolphins. The Dolphins were out of picks. They were done with the draft. Garrett was making calls to potential free agents. He was determining whether Fitzpatrick would be interested in signing with the Dolphins if he made it through without getting selected.

"He was a Princeton guy," Fitzpatrick said. "He's saying, 'Hey, I don't know what's going to happen here in the last few picks, but we'd love to have you in. I like the way you play. I've seen a lot of you.'"

The call-waiting notification sounded before Fitzpatrick could give Garrett an answer. It was the 314 area code. St. Louis was on the clock. The Rams had pick number 250. It was Rams coach Mike Martz.

"We'd love to have you with the Rams," Martz said. "We're going to pick you with this pick."

Fitzpatrick walked into the living room and into quite a celebration. "It was awesome," he said. "I went out there and everybody was so happy. It was just such a sense of relief for me."

He felt wanted. "It's better to be drafted. It's better to have that feeling of being drafted. I'm glad now, looking back at it, that my dad had all those people over. He's usually right about stuff," he said. "I did end up getting drafted, and I did end up being able to share that moment with a lot of people that helped me get there."

Even if he didn't get drafted, even if he didn't make it in the NFL, he still owned a pretty valuable piece of sheepskin. He had a degree from Harvard University.

||||||||||||||||||||||||||||||||||||||||||||||

Ryan Fitzpatrick has been the definition of a journeyman quarterback. He's started for six different teams. He is the only quarterback to start and win a game against one team as the quarterback for five different teams. He has been just good enough to keep getting jobs but played poorly enough that he's been unable to keep them.

In his first twelve years in the NFL, he had a 46-69-1 record as a starter, and he has never played on a team that made the play-offs. Even when it appeared he had found a team to call his home after a strong season, as he did after nearly getting the Jets into the play-offs in 2015, he followed it up with a dreadful season in which he lost his starting job not once but twice.

It hasn't been easy for him or his wife, Liza. She played soccer at Harvard and was a captain her senior year. They met in college and he proposed to her during his rookie season with the Rams after a meal at McDonald's. He used money from their joint account to buy her ring, which he knew drained the resources in it. When she went to use the card at a department store, the salesperson by accident charged her twice, and Liza told the clerk she would check her account on the computer when she got home to make sure the extra charge had been credited back to her. Ryan knew the ring would show up when Liza checked their account online. As a result, he had to give it to her before she saw the transaction in the bank account. He had the engagement ring in their car and gave it to her while she still had sweet-and-sour sauce on her face from her ten-piece order of Chicken McNuggets.

They have six children, each born in a different city. Neither of them ever takes off their wedding ring. Plenty of players have earrings or necklaces on during games, but Fitzpatrick is unique in that his wedding ring remains on his finger. If he threw with his left hand, it would be a problem if his finger was caught in the face mask of a rushing lineman as he was releasing the football. The risk is lower because he's right-handed, but there is still the chance of the ring getting caught in a face mask and doing major damage. He could even lose a finger.

When Fitzpatrick was with the Rams, one of his teammates was veteran quarterback Gus Frerotte, who played with seven teams, and the Vikings twice. His first stop was Washington after the Redskins drafted him in the seventh round in 1994. "You have to understand that in the NFL, once you're a seventh-round pick, you are always a seventh-round pick," Frerotte told Fitzpatrick. "Never forget that."

Fitzpatrick had all the intangibles: great leadership skills, intelligent, well-liked by his teammates. He had good physical skills: very good running ability, better than average arm strength. But his booksmarts didn't always translate onto the football field. Maybe he was just too smart and outsmarted himself instead of the defense. Or maybe reading *War and Peace* was much easier than reading defenses.

He bounced around so much it was dizzying. Two years with the Rams; two years with the Bengals; four years with the Bills; one year with the Titans; one year with the Texans; two years with the Jets; and, in 2017, he signed with the Bucs.

Mike Fitzpatrick hoped his son would have found a home and established himself as a franchise quarterback.

"I accepted it for what it is," he said. "To me, it's such an unbelievable honor he even got to play in the NFL. I look back at his draft class and very few of those guys are even left. I look at it as the glass is half full. I feel for my daughter-in-law and the grandkids. It's tough to change schools."

Mike's son has lived the life of a nomad. His longest stop was in Buffalo. He got off to a red-hot start in 2011 with twelve touchdown passes in the first six games, and the Bills responded by signing him to a six-year $59 million contract with $24 million guaranteed. His play steadily regressed, and he was cut after the 2012 season.

Next stop: Tennessee. Next stop: Houston. Next stop: New York. Next stop: Tampa.

The Jets signed him to back up Geno Smith in 2015, but after Smith had his jaw broken during training camp in a locker-room fight with a teammate over $600, Fitzpatrick became the starter. He exceeded the Jets' expectations and was a bargain at $3.25 million in the second year of a two-year deal he had signed with the Texans. He threw a franchise-record thirty-one touchdowns—sixteen more than Joe Namath had in the Jets' only Super Bowl season in 1968—and the Jets won ten games after winning just four the previous season. But Fitzpatrick threw three interceptions on the Jets' final three possessions of the regular season in Buffalo, and the loss knocked them out of the play-offs.

The good news was that he was a free agent and would be negotiating off his best season. The bad news was that the three interceptions in the fourth quarter in Buffalo scared the Jets and any other team away from offering him a lucrative long-term deal. They did propose a three-year $24 million contract with $12 million in the first year and $3 million of the $6 million in the second year guaranteed. The Jets clearly stated their intentions with their offer: The $12 million in the first year was starter's money, even if it was below market; but the $6 million in each of the last two years was backup money.

Fitzpatrick rejected the offer and missed the entire off-season program. His absence left the Jets with Smith, second-year quarterback Bryce Petty, and rookie Christian Hackenberg. Jets fans pressured management to sign Fitzpatrick, fearing what the season would turn into without him. On the eve of training camp, the Jets and Fitzpatrick compromised, and he signed a one-year contract for $12 million.

Fitzpatrick followed up with a hugely disappointing season. He had twelve touchdowns and seventeen interceptions and threw for 1,200 fewer yards than he did in 2015. The Jets won only five games. Fitzpatrick lost his job to Smith but got it back when Smith tore his ACL; and lost his job to Petty but got it back when Petty was placed on injured reserve with a torn labrum.

Fitzpatrick will keep looking for a job until he makes the decision that he no longer wants to play. Even if he never makes it to the play-offs, Fitzpatrick has squeezed far more out of his career than anybody anticipated. His father thinks he will find a life in football after he is done playing. "It's impossible for me to believe he can walk away from football," he said. "From an analytical point of view, he is way too into the study of it, the understanding of defenses. I told Ryan, 'You're never going to be the greatest quarterback who ever played in the NFL, but you might be the best offensive coordinator the NFL has ever seen.'"

Clearly, the smart genes have been passed down from generation to generation in the Fitzpatrick family. Mike works in one of the largest rocket manufacturing plants in the country. He builds rockets that provide targets for military defense practice runs. Safe to say, football is not rocket science.

When Ryan Fitzpatrick played in Houston in 2014, he brought his oldest son, Brady, just seven at the time, to one of his press conferences. He asked the media to quiz Brady by giving him any two numbers between 90 and 99 and he would do the multiplication in his head.

The numbers 93 and 97 were requested.

Brady thought for a moment.

"9,021," he said.

He has solved a Rubik's cube in less than ninety seconds.

Sounds like another Harvard man.

PHIL SIMMS

Getting His Phil of Football

Christopher Simms was in the stands when his father threw a near-perfect game in Super Bowl XXI at the Rose Bowl in Pasadena, California.

January 25, 1987, was a gorgeous day. The picturesque San Gabriel Mountains provided the perfect backdrop to one of the great performances in NFL history. Phil Simms completed 22 of 25 passes—the 88 percent completion rate is a Super Bowl record—in the New York Giants' 39–20 victory over the Denver Broncos.

"I was six and a half years old, but I was the smartest six-and-a-half-year-old you've ever met when it came to football," Chris said. "I knew every guy on every team."

Chris remembers his father telling him after the game how close he had come to not having one ball hit the ground. "One was pass interference," Chris said. "Two were questionable drops. They would have been good catches, but they certainly could have been caught."

For the little-kid part of Chris, there was the Disney World halftime show. As a football lover, he soaked it all in, watching his father play and then making it down to the field to celebrate after the game. He still remembers going back to the team hotel in Costa Mesa and seeing his father for the first time as a Super Bowl champion. Over the years, Chris has watched the tape of the game more than one hundred times.

"There is nobody who knows that game better than me," Chris said. "If I'm home in New Jersey, I have a little stash of tapes of Dad. If it's 11:30 and I'm going to bed, I might throw in one of those tapes. Instead of watching *SportsCenter*, I'm going to watch a tape of Dad for thirty to forty minutes and relive the good old days."

Chris was the son of a quarterback and became an NFL quarterback himself, although without the success or longevity of his father; and his younger brother Matt became an NFL quarterback as well.

"Dad would always remind me I did have a little bit more of a privileged life," Simms said. "I didn't grow up on a farm. I didn't have to wake up early and throw newspapers around Louisville, Kentucky. I knew I was fortunate that I didn't have to do those things. But it taught me life lessons. Hey, if you want to get somewhere in life, work ethic is extremely important."

Phil's sons worked hard enough to make it to the NFL, even if they were fortunate enough to grow up in a more comfortable environment than their father. The two-story Simms family home in Franklin Lakes, New Jersey, is on nineteen acres, has six bedrooms, a lake, a pool, and a large unattached office that is far bigger than many apartments twenty-five miles away in Manhattan.

It is the goal of every parent for their children to have a better life than they did, especially growing up. Phil Simms's fifteen years in the NFL and his post-football career as the lead analyst for the NFL, first on NBC and then on CBS, provided very nicely for his wife, two sons, and daughter.

When Simms's mother passed away in 2015, the family went to the funeral in Louisville. The Catholic church was only 500 yards from Simms's old house. After the service, they walked over to 1003 Sarah Drive.

"This is where I grew up," Phil said.

It was just a little brick house. His kids were in shock.

"Dad instilled a lot of good values in us early on," Chris said. "People say you grew up with a silver spoon. Yeah, my mom is the daughter of a butcher and my dad is the son of a farmer/factory worker. They really knew how to spoil us. I know he gets angry when people say that."

Phil Simms came from nothing. He was the fourth of five boys in a family with eight children. They lived on his grandfather's tobacco farm in Springfield, Kentucky. His mother had the kids in a hurry. The youngest and the oldest of seven of them are just ten years apart. After Phil completed first grade, they moved to Louisville and lived in a rental for one year before his parents bought a two-bedroom house. Boys in one bedroom sharing two beds, girls in another bedroom, and Barbara and William Simms slept in their own bedroom.

Simms adored his mother. She had a heart of gold, and at

five foot nine she was always self-conscious about her height. His father was an alcoholic. He was into sports and spirits, short on the compliments, and lacked warmth.

There wasn't much money, so as soon as the Simms boys were old enough, they worked. Beginning in the second grade, Phil would help out his oldest brother on his paper route delivering the Louisville *Courier-Journal* until he was old enough to get his own route. One of the perks of being a newspaper delivery boy was the Simms family received a free copy every day.

His son Chris never had a paper route in New Jersey. He often rode his bicycle to school. Phil couldn't ride his bike to do his paper route. It was too hard to maneuver in and out of driveways, and if he cut across the front yards, the customers would complain. He did it all on foot.

"We would wake up at five and we were out the door by 5:05 because you had your clothes laid out," he said. "We would do this whatever the weather was. We would have our paper sacks and would jog to where the papers were dropped off."

The boys would stuff the newspapers in their sacks and then take off in different directions. "If you hustled and really ran, you could be back in the house by 6:10," he said.

Even though Barbara Simms had eight kids, she worked every day. She and her husband left the house for their factory jobs by 6:30. "My sisters all had jobs in the kitchen," Phil Simms said. "You make the oatmeal. You make the eggs. You cook the toast. You clean the table. Somebody had to wash the dishes. Somebody had to dry them. It all had to be done every day, and there was never a day it wasn't done. When my parents got home, if there was something that wasn't done, there was hell to be paid."

The boys would eat breakfast and take a shower, and all eight kids would be off to school.

William Simms set the tone in the house. He had been a tobacco farmer. He smoked a lot. That was not all. "He was an alcoholic," Phil said.

Ten people in a small house with the father a bad drinker. "It was either a bottle or nothing," Simms said. "He was very stern, very tough. He had eight kids in a two-bedroom house. We were like machines. Everybody had jobs. If you wanted something for school, well, good luck. You want new pants and a new shirt? Go get it!"

William Simms would be sober for two months and then drink around the clock for five days straight. "It was tough moments," Phil said.

The father would go on drunken rampages, and Phil thought he planned the tirades so he could storm out of the house and then do whatever he wanted. "I remember standing in the kitchen with two of my brothers, Tommy and David, who were two years apart," Simms said. "Dad was going through one of his rampages and he said something to my mom. My brother David was one of those naturally, extremely, incredibly strong guys. If he grabbed your hand, you'd go, 'Wow. What is that?'"

David was a junior in high school. He had great athletic skill. When Phil would come back to Kentucky in the off-season with the Giants, David would report that he had recently run

two marathons. The next year, he would tell Phil that he squat-
ted 600 pounds.

"He went from a marathon runner to a powerlifter," Phil
said.

The tension was rising in the kitchen in Louisville. "My dad
said something smart to my mom, and my brother David said
something to my dad," Phil said. "He talked back to my dad,
which he would never do."

"Hey, boy," William Simms said.

"Yeah," David fired back.

Silence.

"My dad felt the tone and realized, 'If I carry this any further, I'm going to lose this battle,'" Phil said. "He called my
brother some names and walked out the door."

His drinking never changed the routine in the Simms household. William didn't get violent when he went on his binges, and
the eight kids and Barbara knew to stay away from him when he
was drunk. "I don't know if it was disruptive. Our household was
very independent," Phil said. "Everybody had their role in the
house and out of the house. Did it make it rough on my mother?"

It wasn't easy waiting for her husband to put down the
bottle.

"When you come from a big family like that and everybody is
out doing what they do, you just say, 'Oh, Dad; stay away from him
for a few days. Just go do your job, go to school, do your thing,'"
Phil said. "We were an assembly-line machine that never broke."

Simms didn't wonder when he was a kid why his father felt
compelled to drink. He's thought about it as an adult. "Who

knows? You got eight kids, you're a factory worker, you know how it is at the end of a work week," he said. "I never sat there and thought, 'Why is he like this?' He was tough. His big thing was he wanted you to be as independent as fast as he could get you there, contrary to today's world. None of us raise our kids like that anymore. It's just not part of the world."

William Simms passed away in 1991 after suffering a heart attack. He was just sixty-two years old. "Lived a hard life," Phil said. "He sucked sixty-two years out of it, which was a miracle."

He did not drink his last ten years. "He actually became somewhat of a health nut," Simms said. "We all kind of laughed. It was funny. He bought a bike. It was pretty cool."

William was a very good athlete. He was a pitcher in a time in the farming communities when baseball was everything. He never made it past playing weekend baseball on days off from his job as a farmer before moving to Louisville. He never coached Phil in any sport. Never gave him a pat on the back. Never gave him much encouragement. When you did well, it was expected. When you messed up, he wanted no excuses.

After coming home from a youth baseball game, Phil was eager to tell his father about his accomplishments. He was looking for his father's approval.

"How'd you do today?" William asked.

"I pitched a no-hitter," Phil said.

"You didn't throw too many curveballs, did you?" William said.

"No, I threw a few and hit three home runs," Phil said.

"Yeah? Did you hit them or did you pop them up?" William said.

By the end of the conversation, Phil felt beaten down. He'd had a huge game, but his father refused to let him feel good about it. "By the time he got done, I felt like I failed," he said. "He wasn't a big compliment guy."

It wasn't as if his father was trying to motivate him to play even better. His father didn't think like that. "Like, Jesus Christ, I had a great day and I can't make you happy?" Phil was tempted to say to his father.

Phil Simms has told his children many stories about his life growing up. He is much warmer to his kids than his father was to him. "I do think Dad was very conscious of the way he was brought up and the way his dad treated him on a day-to-day basis," Chris said. "I do think it affected my dad. Not to say his father didn't love him, but he was old-school, and I don't think he necessarily gave a whole lot of compliments toward my dad or his brothers and sisters. My dad was certainly aware of spending time with us when he had time off and making that time count."

Just once, Phil would have loved to have his father tell him how proud he was. One time pull him aside and tell him he did good. Was that too much to ask? Simms knew this was not his father's way and managed not to resent William for it.

"No, no, no, not at all," he said. "I think back, it was almost like [Bill] Parcells. It was 'never be satisfied. Okay, you had a good day, now what's the big deal. Let's go. Come on. You can do better.' That's kind of the same thing. Looking back, it's easier to see."

William let up on Phil as he got older and actually started to attend his baseball games. His future would be in football, but at the time, baseball was where his athletic abilities were taking him. Instead of being critical of Phil's performances, William became more analytical.

The constant refrain the Simms boys heard from their father: Did they want to be ballplayers or just one of those guys who hang out with their friends? What did they plan to do with their lives? It was not a choice most teenagers were prepared to make. Not when they were living in a small house with nine other people. When they hit their teen years, the boys were looking for ways to get out of the house and be with their friends when their parents were sleeping.

"Nothing good happens after midnight" is a common refrain for parents. It was true when Phil escaped from the house with his older brothers Tommy and David. "You hear of Irish twins?" Simms said. "We have Irish triplets."

Tommy was two years older than Phil. David was a year older. The bedroom the five boys slept in was on the second floor, right above William and Barbara's bedroom. On summer nights, once they were confident their parents were sleeping, the boys planned their escape. Tommy was fast and athletic and the smallest of the five boys. He climbed onto the windowsill and pulled up the window. He put his hands behind him and grabbed the top window and braced himself on the sill.

"He just pushed off like he was doing a ski jump to fly over the big bushes that were down below to land in the grass," Phil said. "It would be right outside my mom and dad's window, which would be open at night to get some air. Tommy would roll and stop and stand there to make sure he didn't wake anybody up and he would take off."

David was next. He followed the same routine. Phil played follow the leader. "I wasn't crazy about the jump. I did do it, just like they did," he said. "It was not near as bad as I thought it was."

Before the departure, one of them had to sneak down to the kitchen and unlock the door so they could get back in the house. They would be staying out all night, so they brought their newspaper sacks with them, because they would go straight from partying to delivering the paper. They would then come in through the unlocked kitchen door, eat breakfast, and head back up to bed.

It was the regular summer weekend routine. Phil was playing for the Giants when he went back home to visit his family. The boys started laughing about how they used to jump out the window and were never caught.

"Dad, you never woke up," one of them said.

"You dumb-asses. Of course I heard you jump down from that window. You think I was going to get up to chase you?" William said.

Phil believed his father. "He probably heard us but was thinking, 'I don't give a crap; let them go. If they get in trouble, tough on them.' "

Most of the time, the guys just hung out to pass the time on a hot night. "It was just worthless," Simms said.

But trouble did find them. They climbed fences to work their way into public swimming pools. None of the kids' parents had the kind of money to have a pool in the backyard, and the public pool was the only way to beat the heat at night. One problem: They were trespassing.

"Somebody would report us and the cops would come," Simms said. "We would jump the fence and run. We never got caught. What cop is going to catch a teenager? We would just take off running like crazy. They had no chance of catching us."

It was just harmless fun when the only goal was to cool off. There were times when it got much more intense. A bunch of guys hang out on a street corner, and the conversation inevitably turns to girls. One says something about another's girlfriend or two guys are fighting over the same girl. Fisticuffs would follow. When one of the combatants gave up, the fight would be over.

"That was just a sign of the times. That's all I can say," Simms said. "Unfortunately, fighting was a part of life."

Phil Simms was a big baseball star growing up. Baseball was the big thing in town. There was resentment. That led to his being in his share of fights. "I'm not saying I got into a hundred fights. Of course I didn't," he said. "Just being young, that's part of what it was growing up. I think about it now, what would make you stand off and make you have a fistfight with another person. It's hard to believe that now."

One of Simms's altercations got a little over the top. By the time he arrived home after doing his newspaper route in the morning, his father was sitting in the kitchen waiting for him.

News traveled fast back to the house, and it didn't come in the morning newspaper that Simms delivered. As soon as he saw his father waiting for him, Simms knew this was not going to be good.

"Oh my God, that was about as bad as it got," he said. "He was pretty rough. He didn't hit me, but you could hear it in his voice. It was getting to be that stage of life where, 'Hey, look, you got to decide what you are going to do here, boy.'"

Sports kept Simms out of any more serious trouble. He continued to excel at baseball, and his father started showing up at his games. "I was a really good baseball player. I hate to say things like that, but I was good," he said. "It wasn't uncommon for me in those days in summer baseball when I was fourteen to eighteen years old to play a doubleheader on Sundays, hit a couple of home runs, and pitch a shutout. I would get six or seven hits in a doubleheader easy. I wouldn't even think about it."

He would play summer pickup games when he was in high school. He would bring along his sisters, and when they picked sides, the Simms girls would not be the last ones chosen.

"Everybody in my family could throw, even the girls," Phil said.

What made Simms special as an athlete was the way he could throw the football. He could throw it hard and he could throw it with accuracy. He had only one football scholarship offer as the starting quarterback on his high school team, and that was to Morehead State in Kentucky, 140 miles from Louisville. Indiana and Kentucky offered him baseball scholarships, but it was with the stipulation that he not play football. There was something about football—and particularly about playing quarterback—that was attractive to Simms. Having the ball in his hands every play on offense, playing the mental chess game to outsmart the defense, showing the leadership and preparation that were required.

Wake Forest would have taken Simms and let him play both sports. It never got that far. "It was a random school out of nowhere," Simms said. "The year before they took a running back from my high school. They had seen me my junior year and said, 'Wow, he's interesting.' When Wake Forest told me the requirements in school, I said I wanted no part of that. You have to major in a foreign language and then something else. There's no way. I didn't want to take a foreign language four years in college. I did two years of French in high school. That was it."

Simms didn't get a football offer from Kentucky or Louisville. He went to a big high school, but it had produced just two players who went on to major college programs. Simms threw the ball only ten times a game as a senior, so he wasn't a hot commodity for colleges looking for quarterbacks. He went to Morehead State and redshirted as a freshman and then started four straight years. "I looked at my stats and they were terrible. But there's no denying I could throw," Simms said. "That's all that mattered to the NFL."

Simms decided not to play baseball at Morehead State even though he had permission. The baseball coach was former Yankees left-handed reliever Steve Hamilton, who became known for throwing "The Folly Floater." Hamilton put the hard sell on Simms to play baseball in the spring. "He'd walk by me and go, 'We're waiting on you. Just come by and do a little pitching for us,'" Simms said.

Time constraints prevented him from playing two sports. Even so, Hamilton became his mentor and told him as a freshman he would make it in the NFL. During the summer, Simms would go back to Louisville. He got a job at the Ford plant in town. "It was the greatest thing that ever happened to me," he said.

Phil made money, real money. He was the summer help, so he was given the hardest job in the factory. He had to carry very heavy springs for trucks 20 yards to the assembly line and then put the bolts on that other workers would later secure. It was such hard work that he would sweat through his clothes and his shoes squished when he walked because they were so wet. He had relatives who worked at the plant who would spend their lunch breaks sitting in lawn chairs watching Simms work. "They laughed at me," he said.

The next summer he was laying blacktop.

On May 3, 1979, Simms was the surprise first-round draft pick of the New York Giants. He was the seventh player taken overall. This was way before the days when fans knew every player from Appalachian State to Wisconsin, so most of the draftniks who had filled the ballroom at the Waldorf Astoria Hotel in New York City had no idea who Simms was. Naturally, they booed. NFL Films was caught off guard and wanted to save the moment for posterity. They asked Commissioner

Pete Rozelle to announce the pick again so the fans could boo one more time and this time they could catch it on film. Rozelle had a grin on his face that did not endear him to Simms.

Simms had a rough start to his career with the Giants. One injury after another. By 1983, Bill Parcells had replaced Ray Perkins as the coach, and he selected Scott Brunner to start over Simms. Parcells had not seen much of Simms after he joined the staff in 1981 because he was always hurt. Simms wanted to be traded, but after the Giants were 3-12-1 in '83 and General Manager George Young nearly fired Parcells, the Giants committed to Simms as the quarterback and traded Brunner to the Denver Broncos.

Simms quickly became a "Parcells Guy," as part of the inner circle of the demanding coach. It was considered an honor and quite an achievement to be in that exclusive group. Lawrence Taylor, Harry Carson, George Martin, Maurice Carthon, Jim Burt, Mark Bavaro, and Carl Banks comprised the foundation of the Giants during most of Parcells's eight years as head coach. They were the essence of "Parcells Guys."

Simms had a love-hate relationship with Parcells. The coach knew he could pick on Simms in practice and he could take it, while at the same time the criticism was sending a message to the other players: If Parcells would yell at one of his favorite players, then nobody was immune. Simms handled it, but by the end of the practice he was mentally exhausted from trying to be perfect.

Parcells was a lot like William Simms. Supportive but not full of positive reinforcement. That made Simms comfortable and uncomfortable at the same time. "I'm not going to say he was a father figure. He was my coach," Simms said. "Like all the coaches I've had in my life, he was like my father. They had tremendous similarities. At that time in my life, Bill was the easiest coach I had to deal with. My high school and college coaches would put him to shame. They were just incredible."

In his nineteen years as a head coach with the Giants, Patriots, Jets, and Cowboys, not much changed about Parcells's way of treating his players. Just when they thought he hated them, he showed his softer side and was able to draw them back in.

"He was like a stern father. There was always a moment he made tremendous personal contact," Simms said. "It could be the smallest thing, just patting me on the back as I walked by. I'd go, 'Wow.' Even during a game, every once in a while, he would say something like, 'Phil, way to go.'"

Simms earned Parcells's trust in 1984 when he led the Giants to the play-offs and became the first quarterback in franchise history to throw for 4,000 yards. They were on their way to doing great things together.

In 1987, the Giants won the Super Bowl, with Simms putting on a historic performance. But even that almost wasn't enough for Parcells. The Giants led 26–10 five minutes into the fourth quarter when they had a second and goal at the Denver 1-yard line. Simms then took a 5-yard sack, which infuriated Parcells. On the next play, he threw a touchdown pass to Phil McConkey, which sealed the game. When Simms made it over to the sideline, there was Parcells giving him an earful about the sack. Simms looked at the scoreboard and saw there was 10:48 left in the game and the Giants were up by twenty-three points. "Oh, come on, give me a break," Simms said to Parcells. "I don't want to hear it. The coaching lessons are over for today."

Simms would have loved to share the moment with his parents back at the team hotel in Costa Mesa after the game, but there was so much traffic and it was such a long drive—sixty miles—that his parents couldn't get there. "They're from Kentucky and we were out in Los Angeles," Simms said. "It might have taken them six hours to get to our hotel."

Simms was able to see his parents the next day after he was presented with the Super Bowl MVP Trophy. William Simms was a proud man. The game was the highlight of Phil Simms's professional life. His personal life has been filled with its share of sadness. His brother David and his sister Mary Anne both died from brain cancer way before their time. His father was a young man when he died. His mother died at the age of eighty-two in 2015.

Phil said that David and Mary Anne were the nicest of his siblings. "David was driving to work one day and he started shaking and pulled over to the side of the road," Simms said. "He went to the doctor and didn't go to work. The doctor said, 'Look, I don't know how to tell you this. I got to be honest. Get your life in order. You got six months max to live.' He died almost to the day six months later."

When Simms's father passed away, he was a big Giants fan and a big football fan. His son had finally won his approval.

Phil had learned his father's lesson. "If you're going to do it, then damn it, do it," Simms said.

William Simms's son had made the decision to play ball and not just hang out on Louisville street corners in the summertime.

||||||||||||||||||||||||||||||||||||||||||||||||||

Phil Simms was walking through Newark International Airport on September 24, 2006. He had landed back home on a flight from Pittsburgh after working the Bengals-Steelers game for CBS. He had just been briefed on the physical condition of his oldest son, Chris, the quarterback for the Tampa Bay Buccaneers.

During his fifteen-year career with the Giants, Simms had suffered injuries to his knee, elbow, shoulder, and thumb, all hazards of the trade for a quarterback. But he had never suffered an internal injury. Now he was listening to details about Chris, who was in a Tampa hospital after his spleen was ruptured in a game against the Panthers.

It was unclear at what point in the game he had suffered the injury, but originally it was thought to be just bruised ribs. He was also suffering from dehydration and went into the locker room to get IV fluids. He actually led a fourth-quarter drive that resulted in a field goal that put the Bucs ahead, but the defense couldn't hold the lead and the Bucs lost.

The spleen may have ruptured in the first quarter when Chris was crushed by linebacker Thomas Davis and defensive tackle Kris Jenkins. "Now did my spleen rupture at that point and start bleeding? I don't know that," he said a few weeks later. "But I was in significant pain from that point on. I took a good number of hits after that that I'm sure didn't help the situation."

But he refused to come out of the game. Bucs coach Jon Gruden and the doctors constantly checked up on him, but he kept saying he was fine. "There was nothing they were going to be able to do that day. They weren't going to pull me off," Chris said. "We were struggling. I was the starting quarterback. I didn't see any bone sticking out of my skin and I didn't see blood. So I was going to play. There was no way they were going to get me out of there."

It was a serious situation. Phil never left the airport in Newark. He took the next flight to Tampa. His wife, Diana, also traveled to Tampa. Chris had his spleen removed, and although he later resumed his career with the Bucs and then played for the Broncos and the Titans, his career was effectively over. He played in only four games after the spleen surgery and retired after the 2010 season.

Chris could really throw the football. So could younger brother Matt, who was on the practice squad for the Falcons in their 2016 NFC Championship season. Neither was as good a player as their father. Phil never pressured his sons, although he advises parents now to take a more proactive role in decision making with their sons' careers than he did.

"Parents ask me questions all the time," he said. "I tell them, 'Look, it's your child. You're asking me my opinion. Here's what

I would do. What does your child know? He knows nothing. You're talking about a seventeen-year-old or eighteen-year-old kid. Why are you going to let him decide and tell you? What do they know? You're the parent.' I knew what would be best but I let my sons get too involved in the decision making."

Simms wanted Chris to play football and baseball. He thought he was good enough to be a major-league baseball pitcher. He was left-handed and could throw hard. Chris also played basketball. "I let it go," Phil Simms said. " 'Whatever. All right, play basketball.' I really, really wanted him to play baseball because I knew he was a good player."

Phil was able to see Chris play only four or five high school football games in New Jersey. He was almost always out of town preparing for the Sunday NFL broadcast. "Was I going to stay back and watch a Friday night game? I felt like I was cheating the job," he said.

He wanted Chris to play football at Tennessee, but after first making the decision to follow his father's advice, Chris changed his mind and committed to play at the University of Texas.

By the time Chris was playing youth sports, Phil was a Super Bowl champion and still the starting quarterback for the Giants. There was a lot of pressure that came with being Phil Simms's son, and Chris had just enough swagger to him that he was able to overcome the cutthroat attitude of parents attending games who rooted for him to fail out of jealousy.

"When they would play sports, they would hear the taunts from other parents," Phil Simms said.

He coached his sons' Little League baseball teams in the

spring. He coached Matt's baseball team for four years. "When they would come up to bat, just to see all the moms and dads: 'Oh, strike him out. Strike him out.' Wow, all of a sudden the game became violent," Simms said. "It was really strange. I'm not Pollyanna by any means. [But] I don't understand the cursing at the player. To hear that in Little League games was incredible. We know what people are. Are we ever surprised? Have low expectations and you will never be disappointed."

He was reluctant to attend any of his sons' football practices. He didn't want the head coach to feel he was infringing on his territory. He advised Chris how to deal with Gruden, who was always yelling at him. "He's a father," Chris said. "No father likes to see their kids yelled at a lot by the head coach on television. Dad is a protective father. It probably did bother him a little bit."

Chris's youth football games were not far from their house, and Phil was disturbed the first time he went. "I'd never seen him play. He was a seventh grader," he said. "They were playing a pretty good team and they were winning. Chris got hit and it kind of shook him up and you would have thought the people on the other team had won the million-dollar lottery. It was incredible how much they cheered and went crazy. They were losing 35–0. What do you do? This is not an uncommon story."

Chris Simms would walk into a gym for one of his basketball games when he was ten years old and hear people whispering, "That's Phil Simms's son."

It motivated him.

"Okay, I'm going to show them how good I am today,"

Chris said. "I'm going to whoop everybody's butt and score 35. I almost relished it to a degree more than I felt it put pressure on me. I looked at it as a chance to show off and carry the name a little bit."

Chris and Matt Simms didn't receive the immediate analysis and positive reinforcement from their father after their high school and college football games. Phil did a lot of New England Patriots games when Matt was in high school, so he did try to get home for the Friday night games after doing his work at practice and then drive back to Foxborough on Saturday to meet with the visiting team.

Most of the time, it was not logistically possible to be in New Jersey on Friday nights. It was even more difficult to attend the college games. Chris was at Texas, and later Matt went from Louisville to El Camino College in Los Angeles before he went to Tennessee. Phil would get to the games if he was in the area or had a bye weekend. Texas always played the day after Thanksgiving and Phil always worked Thanksgiving, so he was able to attend the holiday weekend game in Austin.

One of the traditions of college football is the parents all waiting for the players after the game, home or away. Diana Simms traveled to many of the games, but Chris and Matt missed out on having their father there as soon as the game was over.

"You can't have it all in life," Chris said. "It is what it is. Certainly I would have loved for my dad to be there as I walked out of the locker room after a big win against Texas A&M. My dad's career also gave me a lot of memories and other great things in life. I don't lose my perspective on that."

He knew that as soon as the game was over his cell phone would blow up. Phil kept calling until Chris was able to answer the phone. He wanted a rundown on the game and how he played. Sometimes Phil was able to catch twenty minutes on television but still wanted to hear about it from Chris. They would later watch tapes of the game together. Phil was very rarely critical and wouldn't get on him for making a bad decision or throwing the ball into double coverage. His critiques were about technique and throwing motion. "He was always positive," Chris said. "I learned so many good lessons from Dad, not only in life, but how to approach football in general."

But when Simms did manage to make it to one of Chris's games, the kid felt his presence. "When I got to high school and college, I was pretty confident in my abilities," he said. "I knew what I was as an athlete. When I knew Dad was there, I really wanted to impress him. He didn't go to many games and I might have put a little pressure on myself because I wanted to impress my father. That's as far as it went. My dad is my dad, but of course, he's like my best friend in the world, too."

Phil was supportive of Chris when he was arrested in lower Manhattan in July 2010 for allegedly smoking pot while driving with his pregnant wife in the car. He was later found not guilty by a jury that took less than one hour to deliver a verdict. His brother Matt was suspended four games by Louisville in 2008 for marijuana use during his redshirt freshman season.

"I think Dad knew, whether it was me or Matt, when we did something wrong or got in trouble, we were harder on ourselves than anything," Chris said. "Listen, have I been a perfect citizen my whole life? No, I'm not going to say I have been. But that was one night I did nothing wrong and I kind of got wrongly accused and put in a bad situation. They then take my mug shot at 7 a.m. even though I got arrested at 11:15 at night. I slept on a jail room floor. Then they took my mug shot and I looked like crap. But Dad was very understanding of all that. I think he knew in his heart that my brother and I were good people and we try to do the best. We weren't perfect. When you are young and you have money and you are playing football, sometimes you do some stupid things."

The marijuana incident was the beginning of the end of a tumultuous one-year stay for Matt Simms back in his father's hometown. Phil didn't want Matt to attend Louisville. "I grew up there and I wanted to get him out of that atmosphere," he said.

Even before Matt got to Louisville, Phil remembers his son being frustrated with the comparisons to his quarterback father and quarterback brother.

"If I have to hear another word about my dad or my brother, I'm going to knock somebody out," Matt said, kind of half joking.

"Yeah, I know. I'm sorry, son," Phil said.

He decided to attend Louisville over North Carolina, Boston College, and North Carolina State because he wanted to play for Coach Bobby Petrino. After spending two days around the team on a recruiting visit, Phil picked Matt up at Louisville's stadium and his younger son was sold.

Phil glanced over at him in the car and could tell by the look on his face that he had made up his mind. "It's not even close," Matt said. "They are so advanced over everybody else, it's ridiculous."

But before Matt could even step foot on campus, Petrino accepted a job to coach the Atlanta Falcons. After the marijuana incident, he transferred to El Camino and stayed for one year before going to Tennessee. He was recruited to Tennessee—the school his father wanted Chris to attend—by Lane Kiffin, a former NFL head coach with the Oakland Raiders. Kiffin had been at Tennessee just one season when Simms arrived, and it seemed like they could grow together.

"Lane Kiffin wanted him. He thought he was the man," Phil Simms said.

Then Pete Carroll quit at USC to take a job with the Seattle Seahawks. Kiffin had been an assistant under Carroll at USC and Kiffin was hired to replace him, leaving behind a lot of unhappy people. "Matt was there two days and Lane Kiffin left," Phil said. "I should have pulled him out of there. I didn't do it. That was a mistake."

Kiffin brought Matt Simms into his office and apologized.

"Hey, I really feel terrible about this," Kiffin said.

"Hey, Coach, it's a great opportunity," Matt said.

Two major college coaches recruited Matt Simms, and he accepted scholarships each time, but he never got on the field with either one of them. Chris was disappointed when he lasted until the third round of the 2003 draft after he had been led to believe he would be taken in the first round. His brother, Matt, was not drafted at all in 2012 and signed as a free agent with the New York Jets.

Chris never had his 1986 Super Bowl moment. Matt has struggled to find his way onto active rosters. It wasn't easy living up to the accomplishments of their father. Phil wishes things had gone differently for his sons. He wanted Chris to go to Tennessee, two years after Peyton Manning's last season in Knoxville. He of course wishes Chris had never suffered the spleen injury, which could have been fatal. The previous season, Chris started and nearly beat the Washington Redskins in a play-off game. His career was just getting started.

Simms can only wonder what would have happened with Matt if Petrino hadn't left Louisville and then Kiffin hadn't left Tennessee and then Matt had truly been given a fair chance with the Jets, a team that was always searching for a quarterback.

But he's never told his sons he is disappointed in their football careers. Not once.

"I am disappointed," Chris said. "Dad is not disappointed. I'm sure he feels I got a tough break. I did, but I've had a lot of really other fortunate things go on in my life and I try not to lose sight of that. I was a realist and knew it might be really tough to have the same career as my father. I only got eight years. He got fifteen."

Chris just couldn't get his career back on track after the spleen injury. Not only is he left to wonder how good he might have been, but his father has to live with that, too. "Once Christopher lost his spleen, I'm not saying his career ended, but by the time he recovered, the league was ready to give up on him. It took a long time to recover," Phil said. "He was never the same person physically until three or four years later. He hung in there for a few years."

Phil regrets that Chris was injured and he regrets that Matt has never received a chance to prove he can be a starting quarterback in the NFL. "One thing I would definitely say is both of them are absolutely and were NFL-caliber athletes to play quarterback and to do well," Phil said. "I never doubted that. It's not just because they are my sons. It's just a fact."

Chris knows everything about his father's career. Matt is learning along the way. When Phil presented him with the watch he was awarded for being the MVP of the 1986 Pro Bowl, Matt's reaction was typical.

"Thanks, Dad. Damn, you were the MVP in the Pro Bowl?" Matt said.

"You didn't know that?" Phil said.

"I didn't," Matt said.

"Holy Christ, son," Phil said.

Chris never had the opportunity to get himself established. If he feels cheated, it's just that he was never able to prove he could play and how good he was. "I don't think people ever realized I had legit talent," he said.

He has followed his father into the football broadcasting business. Matt is still trying to make it in the NFL. Even though he was on the Falcons practice squad and did not get to dress for the game, Phil and Diana were in the stands at NRG Stadium for the Super Bowl in 2017.

It was thirty years after Phil had put on the greatest performance of his life in Super Bowl XXI when he threw a near-perfect game.

JOE FLACCO
Taking No Flack

Joe Flacco gets in his car at the Baltimore Ravens facility and hits speed dial for his father, Steve, on his cell phone.

It's a twenty-minute drive from Owings Mills, Maryland, to Flacco's home. He grew up as the oldest of six kids, with four brothers and a sister, and he now has three sons and a daughter of his own who were born within the first five years he was married. He knows the tumult that awaits when he walks in the door. As a result, the best time to talk to his father is when he's alone in the car, and he makes the call every other day.

Joe wants to talk anything but football. That's all Steve wants to talk about.

"I got to try and get him off topic, just to talk about something normal," Joe said. "I usually do not want to talk football. I talk football all day. I'm his son, he's very interested in what's going on, so he loves to talk football. I got to tell him to shut up."

Flacco laughs telling this story. He's in a conference room

next to the cafeteria at the Ravens offices. In a few minutes, he will sit at a table and have lunch with John Harbaugh, the Ravens coach. They won a Super Bowl together at the end of the 2012 season and Flacco was the Super Bowl MVP.

Joe and Steve Flacco are very close, almost like brothers. He knows his father needs his football fix and that he wants to know about his son's surgically repaired knee, about the Ravens' next opponent, about where the season is going. Flacco concedes that it's a lost cause trying to steer the conversation away from football. Steve can't get enough of it, and he's always been opinionated.

"I'm usually bitching," Steve said. "Constantly complaining, always critical. I'm always asking him questions. A lot of times we're as bad as the people he meets in the street. Either he doesn't know the answers or he doesn't want to be bothered by it."

Steve Flacco knows enough that Joe respects his football knowledge. Steve Flacco was a running back at the University of Pennsylvania. In the Ivy League title game against Harvard in 1982, the Quakers held a 20–0 lead going into the fourth quarter. But the Crimson stormed from behind with three touchdowns and grabbed a 21–20 lead with 1:28 left. Penn started its drive at its own 20. The Quakers had a long way to go with not a lot of time to do it. They were moving the ball.

Penn had not won the Ivy title in twenty-three years. Steve Flacco had a crucial 10-yard catch-and-run and managed to get out of bounds with three seconds remaining, positioning Penn to kick a 38-yard field goal to win the game. According to an account of the game years later by the *Philadelphia Daily News*, the field goal was wide left, but Harvard was called for a questionable roughing the kicker penalty. Penn took advantage and kicked a 27-yard field goal to win the game on the final play.

"I definitely knew he was a very good athlete," Joe said. "When I was a young kid, you could tell he was an athletic guy."

Joe feels comfortable discussing football strategy and the behind-the-scenes issues he must deal with as the quarterback and leader of the team. "You are about the only one they can really talk to and be close with when things are going good or bad," Steve said. "Obviously, you're close with them forever, including now. One of the things people don't realize is the level of stress that comes with that job on a daily basis. Sometimes, it's as simple as being able to call your dad and just talk about something else or vent about things that are bothering you. It's a huge help psychologically."

Joe was able to find some old videos of his father playing at Penn, but it's not like when Eli Manning went to Ole Miss, his father Archie's school, and looked through the media guide and saw his father's achievements on just about every page. Steve Flacco's football career was slowed by a bunch of injuries and he didn't play a lot. The highlight was the play against Harvard.

"He had a couple of videos and there's some old pictures and my mom's scrapbooks," Joe said. "So you would be able to go back and look through some old articles about him and his playing days."

Joe Flacco didn't start playing organized football until the seventh grade, and he didn't play quarterback until he was a freshman in high school. Flacco was interested in being a running back, but his father convinced him there would be better opportunities for him to get on the field as a quarterback. He had an ability to really throw the ball. He would grow to six foot six inches, way too big for a running back. Too easy to hit. His father gave him good advice.

Steve Flacco had started his own mortgage broker business with friends when Joe was twelve and worked much of the time from their home in Audubon, New Jersey. He was around when Joe and his brothers returned home from school, and there was hardly a day that went by when they weren't throwing the ball around.

"My dad never coached me," Flacco said. "I don't think he ever wanted to, and I was happy. We did so much in the backyard, and we grew up two doors from our grade school, which had a big schoolyard, and we'd always go to the park. We were constantly getting together with my uncle and my brothers and him. We were going to the field and hitting baseballs and then we'd go on the field and throw the football around. He wasn't ever directly my coach, but he taught me football and baseball. I played basketball in high school, but he's a terrible basketball player so he didn't teach me any of that."

Flacco was a three-sport athlete at Audubon High School, playing football, baseball, and basketball. He was an intimidating presence on the mound as a pitcher. If he had a future in professional sports, it was going to be in football. But Audubon was a small school, with only 165 students in Joe's graduating class in 2003. That worked against him in recruiting. His team also wasn't very good.

"My best year was my junior year. We went 5-5," he said. "My sophomore year we were 2-8. My senior year we were 4-6. So we were never a good football team."

They barely had enough guys to put together a team. Including freshmen, they had only forty players. "Most of us played two ways," he said. "There were probably one or two guys that didn't play on both sides. I would play safety on defense."

Steve worked hard trying to get Joe ready for college football. He would show up at the end of practice around 5:30 p.m. every day.

"The thing about him is after practice he would usually come by with one of my brothers and I would get extra throwing in," Flacco said. "Because we were a small school, we would practice defense one day, offense the next day. We wouldn't get a ton of throwing in."

His younger brothers videotaped the games, and Joe would then study them with his father. The coaches were not grading the tapes and there was no critical review, which led to the Flaccos doing that themselves after they got home from the Friday night games. It helped Flacco begin to see the entire field. His father was able to turn his dissection of negative plays into learning experiences. He was not one of those fathers who would sit in the stands and try to coach the team from a distance. It could be frustrating, especially because the team was not very good.

"Our games were usually pretty exciting," Steve said. "Joe never played on a winning team in high school, but we always had the capability to score on teams because he would make that happen by throwing the ball. We weren't going to run the ball on anybody. He was always running for his life."

The team was not physical and they had a hard time protecting Flacco. "The better teams would just beat the hell out of us," Steve said. "There were games we would get him home and his undergarments would be torn off underneath his jersey and pads. Fortunately at that age, he was so flexible."

His father remembers some plays ended with Joe sitting on his butt, his legs spread out and his head pressed to the ground with defensive players sitting on top of him. "He took some serious beatings," he said.

Regardless of how he played, Joe could always count on support from his father. "One of the greatest things about playing was coming home to him," Joe said.

There were times when Steve and his other four sons would gang up on Joe and make fun of him after a game to lighten the mood. "They would razz you and stuff like that," Joe said. "At the same time, they would always have a good spin on it. He'd always bring it back and make you feel good about the way things went or the way things are going to go."

Steve is five-eleven. His wife, Karen, is five-six. By Joe's senior year in high school, he was already six foot five, but he weighed only 205 pounds. "It freaked us out, he was still growing," Steve said.

The center on the football team was just five foot eight, and Joe had to position himself in a baseball catcher's squat to take the snap. "He looked like a man with his little kids around him in the huddle," Steve said.

One thing stood out. Flacco could sling the football.

"I said to him, 'You know what, Joe? There are very few people who can throw a football the way you do right now,'" Steve said. "I'm not talking about arm strength. I'm talking about control. People get wrapped up in arm strength. It's how you control the ball. The amount of pace you put on the ball. You want the ball to get to a certain point at a certain time, sometimes from a certain angle. He had the ability at a very early age to do that. Part of that was most of the time we played against defensive backs that were more athletic than our receivers. So he learned at an early point that when and where the ball was thrown was a lot more important than who it was thrown to. There was a lot more to it than just, 'Okay, we're going to hit this guy.' It was like, we were going to fake the ball into the line and he was going to pop up and the receiver was going to be running open down the sideline. That was very infrequent."

It was a long way from Audubon High School to standing on the podium in the middle of the Superdome holding the Vince Lombardi Trophy with confetti floating down from the rafters onto Joe Flacco's head following Super Bowl XLVII in 2013. It was a circuitous route filled with much aggravation and frustration.

|||||||||||||||||||||||||||||||||||||||||||||||||

It was a wild Super Bowl. The lights went out, and the Ravens nearly blew a 28–6 lead but survived a last-minute chance at the goal line by the 49ers that would have won the game. Instead, the Flaccos were down on the field at the Superdome celebrating, soaking in the atmosphere.

"We were pretty euphoric at that point," Steve said. "It's surreal."

Joe had told his father before the game that he didn't know if he would ever be able to watch football again if he didn't win a Super Bowl. Quarterbacks are defined by their Super Bowl rings. Not only did Joe get a ring, but Roger Goodell presented him with the Super Bowl MVP trophy the morning after the game.

Now flash back to New Jersey and Flacco playing for a bad team at a small high school but wanting to play big-time college football. He had the arm. He had the smarts. He had the desire. He just didn't have a lot of schools after him.

Flacco knew he could play. Did anybody else? "I think my father probably always thought I was pretty good, and so did I," Joe said.

That was validated going into his junior year of high school. He went to a football camp at Rutgers University, and before the season started he was offered a scholarship by Rutgers coach Greg Schiano. "He hadn't even been there for a season yet," Flacco said.

The Flaccos were naive about how to go about getting Joe recruited. "I just thought you were good in high school and you went to a college and that's how you did it," Joe said.

Steve had been prepared, helping Joe during his high school career, but they left it up to Joe's coaches to get the word out with game tapes and highlight films. "Looking back, I probably could have got more recruited if I had gone to more camps, but

I really wasn't willing to do it," Joe said. "I just didn't want to do it. I was doing so many other things in high school. I played football. I played basketball. I played baseball. In the summer, I was doing all those things. I was usually playing a little bit of baseball, so I wasn't really willing to go spend a week at a football camp just so they could offer me [a scholarship]. I thought I had enough out there that they could offer me based on what I had done on the field."

Steve regrets not fully understanding how important the summer camps were in the recruiting process. "We were just dumb," he said. "We don't come from an area that is very heavily recruited. I think Joe was the only kid to come out of his high school in thirty-plus years who played Division I football."

He felt that Joe's high school coaches didn't talk him up enough. "They were just as happy to bury you," he said. "It was very difficult to get him recruited."

Joe had offers from some Mid-American Conference schools, but the ones he seriously considered were from Pittsburgh, Rutgers, and Central Florida. Virginia Tech offered him a scholarship, but they also had one on the table to Marcus Vick, Michael's younger brother. That was enough to turn off Flacco. He leaned on his father for advice and then made his decision: Pittsburgh.

Pitt's coach was Walt Harris, who had been a quarterbacks coach in the NFL and had a solid reputation. "It was by far Joe's best offer," Steve said. "Walt ran one of the most complex, diversified passing games. We were happy to have him playing with Walt."

Those good feelings didn't last long when the Flaccos realized Joe's path to the field was blocked. "When we got him up there, there was no chance he was going to play," Steve said.

He didn't get an opportunity to compete with senior starter Rod Rutherford. Flacco was redshirted as a freshman in 2003. Steve asked Harris if he had recruited his son because he needed a backup and because they lived far enough away in New Jersey and would not be aware of the quarterback depth chart.

"Look, Steve, I recruited a lot of kids who were not on anybody's radar, and we've played them," Harris said.

"That may be true, but it's not the same as a quarterback where you are going to play one guy," Flacco said.

Flacco went into spring camp in 2004 hoping for a chance to compete. Rutherford had an excellent season in 2003, throwing for 3,649 yards with thirty-seven touchdowns and fourteen interceptions. But his eligibility was up. Flacco was going to have to beat out Tyler Palko, who was a year ahead of him, had played a bit as a freshman, and then been redshirted his sophomore year.

"Tyler was so bad they had to leave Rod Rutherford in there the year before at quarterback rather than play him. They redshirted him. As a sophomore," Steve said.

Harris picked Palko to start and named Flacco the third-team quarterback behind Palko and Luke Getsy. But Getsy transferred to Akron when Harris named Palko the starter a few days before the 2014 season opener. That elevated Flacco to second-string, and he played in just three games and threw only 4 passes. The Flaccos were so disgusted after Joe didn't get into a game that they attended against Ohio University, they decided they were done. They stopped driving to the games.

"Against Nebraska, Tyler throws two pick sixes in the first quarter and they stick Joe in the damn game," Steve said. "He gets a first down, then they get a 5-yard penalty and they have Joe quick-kick. He's never punted in his life. They short-snap the ball and he gets the kick off."

In the next-to-last game of the season, Flacco came in against South Florida and completed one pass for 11 yards. It was his only completion in his career at Pitt. The Panthers finished 8-4 and were twenty-fifth in the final Associated Press poll. Palko had a very good season with twenty-four touchdowns and seven interceptions. He was the first visiting quarterback to throw five touchdowns at Notre Dame Stadium. He also tossed five touchdowns against South Florida, earning Pitt a berth in the Fiesta Bowl, where they lost to Utah. Flacco was disgruntled at his lack of playing time.

Harris was fired after the season and replaced by Pittsburgh native Dave Wannstedt, a former Pitt linebacker and the former head coach of the Chicago Bears and Miami Dolphins. "That was a debacle for us," Steve Flacco said. "I actually talked to Dave very early on before Joe got back to campus in the spring."

He complained about how Harris refused to use Joe. Wannstedt assured him there would be no depth chart going into spring ball and everybody would have a chance to compete. Flacco was clearly fighting from behind.

"We got the whole spring. Let's see what happens," Steve told Joe.

Wannstedt brought in former Pitt quarterback Matt Cavanaugh as his offensive coordinator.

"Dad, Matt has to stop practice to calm Tyler down. He threw three or four interceptions in drills," Joe said.

In the first scrimmage of the spring, Flacco threw for 235 yards against Pitt's first-team defense playing with the second-team offense, even though he told his father, "My right tackle doesn't want to block the left end because he's afraid of him."

It became clear that Flacco was not making any progress in taking away Palko's job. He had to find a way to play, and it wasn't going to happen at Pitt. He consulted with his father, and they decided the best thing was to transfer. Steve was as frustrated as Joe. It's something any parent can relate to when their son or daughter is not getting what they believe is deserved playing time, whether it's on a Little League baseball team, a youth soccer team, in Pop Warner football, or in college football. Parents want the best for their children.

"I talked to my father pretty much every day, so I talked to him a lot about that. He had his thoughts and I had my thoughts," Flacco said. "Really, at the end of the day, it was a good thing for me to get out of there because I wanted to play. I didn't want to sit around and wait for something bad to happen to somebody. You expect [Palko] to finish his career. I just wouldn't have played very much at Pitt. I wanted to go play for a couple of years at least."

Flacco asked Wannstedt to release him from his scholarship. Without a release, schools could not recruit him to transfer. He had to initiate all the contact. "The tough part of it was nobody really knew who I was," he said. "Nobody's really technically allowed to reach out to you because I was still under scholarship to Pittsburgh. So you have to start reaching out to people and it's just a real sticky situation. If I was a more highly recruited person and people actually cared that I was leaving Pitt, it might have been a little easier to transfer."

Delaware had recruited Flacco a little bit out of high school, and one of his coaches at Audubon had been coached by Delaware coach K. C. Keeler when he was at a Division III school.

Joe wanted to transfer to Delaware, and Delaware wanted him. Because Delaware is one level down from Pitt, if Flacco could get his release, then he would not have to sit out one year. Wannstedt wasn't even the coach who had recruited Flacco to Pitt, but he still refused to let him go. "The chancellor at Delaware University couldn't believe it. He actually called the chancellor at Pitt. They told him, 'Screw you, we're not releasing you,'" Steve Flacco said. "It was very vindictive. Spiteful."

He left Pitt anyway and enrolled at Delaware. It wasn't as if Flacco was trying to transfer to rival Penn State. He was going to Delaware, a Division I Football Championship Subdivision program. Villanova and James Madison were their big games. "Who knows what the factors were," Joe Flacco said. "I don't really care to think about it anymore. It's not a big deal."

Delaware could not put Flacco on scholarship until he was released from his Pitt scholarship. In January, after the 2005 season, Flacco again asked Pitt to release him. He had already been at Delaware for a semester. Pitt still refused. Joe had to pay his own way for one year. "Fortunately, it was the easiest twenty-grand check I ever wrote in my life," Steve Flacco said. "I hate to spend money. I was so pissed off I wrote those damn tuition checks and loved it."

Pitt was just 5-6 in Wannstedt's first year. Palko's touchdowns dropped to seventeen, and his interceptions went up to nine. He would not get drafted in 2007 and bounced around the National Football League, the Canadian Football League, and the United Football League before finally starting four games for the Kansas City Chiefs in 2011. He had one victory, two touchdowns, and four interceptions and was out of football.

At Flacco's Super Bowl game following the 2012 season, the *Pittsburgh Post-Gazette* spoke to Cavanaugh about what happened with Flacco at Pitt. "I have no reservations about how it played out," he said. "It would be pure speculation to say that we would have been better with Joe."

After sitting out the 2005 season—he had already had missed the 2003 season as a redshirt—Joe Flacco became the starter at Delaware with two years of eligibility remaining. His parents were back in business attending games. The campus in Newark, Delaware, was only forty-five minutes from their house. "It worked out to be good," Steve said. "Part of it was their defense wasn't very good. We constantly had to have our foot on the pedal on offense."

Flacco suffered a knee injury his junior year. It didn't turn out to be serious, but the coaches revamped the offense, put Flacco in the shotgun, and protected him by not having him run the ball.

"They had a great program," Steve Flacco said. "It was a

great time for Joe to be there. The stadium was filled up with twenty-three thousand people. It seemed like more because it was full. It was a really nice place to play. It allowed us to see a lot of games, which was nice."

The Blue Hens were 5-6 in Flacco's first season. He threw eighteen touchdowns and ten interceptions. After the season, Flacco walked into Keeler's office. Flacco had led his high school to the state baseball championship, and his father believes if he'd stuck with it, he would be throwing 95-mile-per-hour fastballs. Flacco asked Keeler if he would allow him to play baseball at Delaware. Keeler didn't think it was a great idea since Flacco was going to be drafted by an NFL team the next year. Flacco had no idea NFL teams considered him a prospect. He scrapped the baseball idea.

The Blue Hens improved to 11-4 in his second year, and he threw twenty-three touchdowns and five interceptions.

Three years after getting beaten out by Tyler Palko in Pittsburgh, football life was good for Joe Flacco. He had resurrected his career. Now the question was, How would NFL teams evaluate him, coming from a lower division of football and playing against lesser competition? Four quarterbacks had previously been drafted from Delaware. The most successful was Rich Gannon, who was a fourth-round pick of the New England Patriots in 1987. He had his best year in 2002, his sixteenth year in the NFL, when he led the Oakland Raiders to the Super Bowl and was named the MVP of the regular season when he threw for 4,689 yards with twenty-six touchdowns and ten interceptions. He was awful in the Raiders' 48–21 loss in the Super Bowl against his former Oakland coach, Jon Gruden, who seemed to know everything that was coming. Gannon had two interceptions returned for touchdowns.

Gannon's overall productive career coming out of Delaware worked in Flacco's favor. But who was going to take him? How high was he going to be drafted?

|||||||||||||||||||||||||||||||||||||||||||

By the time the draft arrived, Flacco had shot up the rankings around the league. He had become one of the top quarterback prospects. The bad memories of Pitt were packed in a box and put through a shredder. He had taken a step down in quality of play to attend Delaware, but it could not have worked out better. After throwing just four passes at Pittsburgh, he had 938 attempts in two seasons at Delaware. He completed 63.4 percent with forty-one touchdowns and just fifteen interceptions. In his second year, he won three play-off games before losing in the Football Championship Subdivision championship game to Appalachian State. In 2009, Delaware placed six twenty-foot-by-thirty-foot posters of its past football stars to the side of the Fightin' Blue Hens stadium. Flacco was one of the six.

It's at times like these that it's easy to reflect on all the people who have helped contribute to the process. There were a lot of kids in the Flacco house. They kept Joe grounded. It was his father who never stopped believing in him.

Keeler once told a funny story to the *Los Angeles Times* that accentuates Flacco's low-key demeanor, so low-key that Steve once called him "dull."

"I remember saying to him, 'Joe, just one time, throw a big touchdown pass in Delaware Stadium, run down the sideline pounding your chest, pointing into the stands,'" Keeler said. "And he'd get flustered: 'Aw, no! I could never do that!' I'd say, 'Why?' And he'd say, 'My parents and my brothers would just tear me up after the game.'"

Flacco is the oldest of five boys. His brother Mike is two years younger than him, and at six-five, he's one inch shorter. Then sister Stephanie is another two years younger and then another two years to John, two years to Brian, and two years to Tom. "My sister kind of separates me and my one brother from the other three," Joe said. "We're still pretty close. It's just me and my brother who is right underneath me; we grew up playing, doing everything together."

Joe and Mike even played on the same Little League baseball team together. They shared a room, and it was not unusual for Steve to have to intervene if things got a little rough. "I definitely remember some times when he had to come in and either throw him off me or throw me off him," Flacco said. "Whatever it is, I was the older brother. I was pretty quiet, went about my business. You usually win things when you are two years older. He's a little bit more aggressive, and he takes things a little bit harder. He wanted to win and he felt like he could compete with me. He would end up a lot of the time getting pretty pissed."

When did those battles stop? Did they ever stop?

"Probably when I got to junior high," he said.

Most of his brothers were athletic. Mike played minor-league baseball in the Baltimore Orioles system, and when that didn't work out as planned, he went to the University of New Haven to play tight end and spent time on the practice squads of San Diego and Jacksonville. John was a walk-on receiver at Stanford. Tom is a quarterback at Western Michigan who was a backup his first two seasons. He was an excellent high school baseball player and was drafted in the thirty-second round by the Phillies in 2014.

Tom is six inches shorter than Joe and not nearly the same prospect, but it never hurts to learn from a brother who is an NFL quarterback. "Joe really keeps his cool; he's really able to keep his cool," Tom told mlive.com. "I think he's a great leader...and I think the way he controls himself on the field— and he's very poised—I think that's what my brother Joe really has and I think that's something that I'm trying to grow and become...that aspect of my game."

Steve Flacco thinks very highly of his kids. He believes Joe is the best quarterback in the NFL. He believes Tom has great potential. "He's Joe Flacco in Michael Vick's body," he said. "When they let him play, they are not going to be able to stop him."

NFL Draft Day 2008: Flacco was back home in Audubon. He was hesitant to watch on television because he didn't know if he was going to be selected in the first round or the fourth round. Against his better judgment, he let ESPN cameras into the house. "I was just sitting on the couch in the living room, waiting anxiously," he said.

Boston College's Matt Ryan was rated as the best quarterback in the draft. He was a consideration for the top overall pick by the Miami Dolphins, but they decided to take Michigan tackle Jake Long. The Falcons selected Ryan third overall. The Ravens were picking eighth and had a mandate from owner Steve Bisciotti to move up to get Ryan. The Rams wanted two first-round picks and second- and third-round picks to trade out of the top spot. The Ravens had Ryan evaluated as the best quarterback and third-best player overall in the draft and Flacco as the second-best quarterback and the number 15 prospect. They wisely didn't make the trade with the Rams, who were asking for too much, and instead moved back to the twenty-sixth spot and then back up to the eighteenth and took Joe Flacco.

"We decided it was time to pull the trigger on the quarterback that we felt was the guy to lead our football team into the future," Ravens general manager Ozzie Newsome said.

If the Eagles, Giants, or Jets were not going to take him, the next closest team within driving distance was the Ravens. Karen Flacco was the most excited of the Flacco crew. Relatively speaking, her son would be playing around the corner.

Suddenly, Joe didn't mind the ESPN cameras.

"I ended up getting picked pretty high, so it all ended up working out pretty well," he said.

The next day Flacco drove down to Baltimore with his parents; his girlfriend, Dana (now his wife); and a couple of his siblings.

Baltimore had a history of being a burial ground for

quarterbacks. Even in 2000, when the Ravens won the Super Bowl, they did it despite having Trent Dilfer as the quarterback for most of the season. In Dilfer's first start, the Ravens didn't score a touchdown. It was the third straight game they didn't get into the end zone and the fourth time that season.

Dilfer became a free agent after the Super Bowl season, and the Ravens had no interest in bringing him back. They changed quarterbacks too often to have any sustained success despite having a shutdown defense led by Ray Lewis. The Ravens were counting on Flacco to change the narrative. He got his chance immediately after Troy Smith and Kyle Boller suffered preseason injuries. Even though he was making the jump from Division I FCS—Steve McNair was the only other first-round quarterback from that level when it was called Division I-AA—and some draft experts thought the Ravens drafted him a round too early, Joe was ready to play.

"When they picked him number 1, you know at some point, it may not be right away, they are going to put the ball in your hands," Steve said. "It's your turn; you are going to get a shot to play. That was a pivotal moment."

He had a really strong family structure to rely on growing up, and now they were going to be able to attend all his home games in Baltimore. That was such a bonus. For most of his growing-up years, Joe's father worked from home and was around to pitch to him in the batting cage in the backyard or throw around the football. His mom took care of all of them.

"My mom was my mom," Flacco said. "She raised a helpless

husband and a bunch of helpless kids. It's a tough job that you get no credit for. We never acknowledge that she did anything for us, but she did everything and made sure everything was great and that we were always taken care of."

She went to all of Joe's games in high school and then at Delaware. Sitting in the stadium on game days in Baltimore is tough on Flacco's mother. The buildup is just as bad.

"My first couple of years in the league she would start getting sick to her stomach on Tuesday, Wednesday, for the Sunday game," Joe Flacco said. "She was just so worried about people picking on her son. She just wants us to do well and win the game and wants the game to be over. Then she can relax for probably a day and a half before she starts getting sick to her stomach again. I'm her boy and she's worried about what people are going to say about me if I do play bad or we don't win."

Flacco became the first quarterback since the 1970 merger to win a play-off game in each of his first five seasons. His seven career play-off victories on the road are the most in NFL history. He is not intimidated by playing in front of hostile crowds, but if the Ravens had had a better record during the regular season, they would have played more home games.

After Flacco's first two years with the Ravens, he spent his downtime in the off-season back in his old bedroom he had shared with his brother. "It's probably more common than you think within our locker room," Joe said.

His parents were happy to have him from the time the Ravens finished their season until the off-season program started. Flacco was not yet married. "He came home to decompress," Steve said. "He would lie on the sofa and let his mom take care of him for a little bit."

The bedroom was decorated with posters and pictures from *Sports Illustrated* and *ESPN* magazine of Barry Sanders, Muhammad Ali, Joe Montana, Steve McNair, Randy Moss... and Tom Brady. The room has remained unchanged. So even when Flacco visits his parents' house now and goes into the bedroom, the picture of Brady is still on the wall. "What do I care?" Flacco said.

It was put up in 2001 when Flacco was in high school and Brady was in his first year as the Patriots' starter, and since then Flacco has faced Brady four times in the play-offs, beating him twice. "I'm sure he doesn't have me hanging on his childhood bedroom wall," he said.

Locker rooms around the NFL are filled with stories of players who were raised in single-parent homes without the stability Flacco enjoyed in his life. Although he says, "We're definitely crazy in our own way," he never takes his upbringing for granted.

"I have no idea how some of the guys that grew up the way they did get as far as they have," he said. "I know how big an influence my parents had on me, and I don't know what I would do without them. I was definitely fortunate to grow up with a mom who stayed at home and cared for us. I hope that I'd still have been the person that I am today without them, but at the same time, you just don't know. There are a lot of rough things along the way. There are a lot of big decisions that I wouldn't have wanted to make by myself as a fourteen-, sixteen-, eighteen-, or even twenty-five-year-old. You want to be able to rely on somebody that you really, really trust."

Steve Flacco imparted one bit of advice to Joe that he always carries around with him: Believe you are the best. "He would always ask us who was the best," Flacco said. "If we didn't immediately say, 'I am,' he was dogging us."

Flacco was the best quarterback in the world for the month of January and the first Sunday of February in 2013. He threw one of the most memorable touchdown passes in play-off history when the underdog Ravens played in Denver in the divisional round after they had defeated the Texans in the wild-card round. Flacco heaved a 70-yard touchdown to Jacoby Jones with 31 seconds left to send the game into overtime, which the Ravens wound up winning. The next week, the Ravens went into New England and beat the Patriots. Flacco outplayed Peyton Manning and Tom Brady in back-to-back games on the road.

He beat the 49ers in the Super Bowl. In the four play-off games, Flacco threw 11 touchdown passes and no interceptions. Then, before all the Flaccos knew it, the confetti was on its way down.

He soon would sign a six-year $120 million contract. In 2016, he would sign a three-year $66 million extension. Between the two deals, there was $96 million guaranteed.

Steve is low-key like Joe, and father and son didn't get emotional when they saw each other for the first time after the Super Bowl. Steve just knew it had been a long road from Audubon to New Orleans with stops in Pittsburgh and Delaware.

He watched and worried for years that the Ravens' strong defense would be wasted if the front office didn't put some offensive weapons around his son.

That night in New Orleans he worried no more. His son was a champion.

JOE MONTANA
Joe Cool Dad

Tom Brady was sitting in the stands with his parents at Candlestick Park in San Francisco for the 1981 NFC Championship Game against the Dallas Cowboys.

He was just four and a half years old, and, like a lot of kids in the Bay Area, Joe Montana was his football hero. At the exact moment Montana threw an off-balance and improbable game-winning touchdown pass to Dwight Clark as he was backpedaling away from Ed "Too Tall" Jones, the man sitting in front of little Tommy Brady stood up and blocked his view of one of the most dramatic catches in NFL history. Brady started to cry. They were not tears of happiness to celebrate the 49ers advancing to their first Super Bowl; the little guy was upset that he missed "the Catch." His mother had to pick him up and console him.

Just as improbable as Montana's acrobatic throw and Clark's amazing catch was that the little boy from San Mateo who was crying would go on to surpass Montana as the greatest quarterback of all time. Montana could not have done much more in his fifteen-year career. He won all four Super Bowls he played in with the 49ers and threw eleven touchdowns and no interceptions. Brady won his fifth championship with the New England Patriots in February 2017 in the seventh Super Bowl he played. Montana's and Brady's football skills were similar, their demeanors very much the same.

It can be argued whether players should be considered heroes or role models or whether that is a job that belongs to parents. Brady had both: Montana was his hero on the field; his father, Tom Sr., was his hero off the field. Tom Sr. always said his three daughters, who played varsity sports in college, and his son, the youngest of the four, who was the quarterback for the University of Michigan, received their athletic genes from their mother, Galynn, who was a competitive athlete into her forties. Tom Sr.'s favorite sport to play is golf.

Tom Brady became the new Joe Cool. Unfortunately for Montana, the Super Bowl torch was not passed to either one of a couple of other Bay Area kids who were also quarterbacks and grew up in his house.

Nathaniel Montana was born in October 1989, almost four months before his father won his fourth Super Bowl. Nicholas Montana, the youngest of Jennifer and Joe's four children, was born in April 1992, during the off-season before his father's last year with the 49ers. Joe then finished his career with two seasons in Kansas City. Brady didn't have to worry about living up to the name on the back of his jersey. His father didn't play football. But the Montana boys faced the pressure of trying to follow in the career footsteps of one of the greatest players in NFL history. During their youth football days, Nate and Nick Montana decided to wear their mother Jennifer's maiden name, Wallace, on their jerseys in an attempt to carve out their own identities.

Imagine Nate walking on at Notre Dame, where his father was a legend, and Coach Charlie Weis assigning him jersey number 16, the number the 49ers retired in his father's honor. Weis told him it was the only quarterback jersey available. Thanks, Coach. Well, at least Weis, a student at Notre Dame when Joe was the quarterback, didn't give him number 3, which Montana made famous in South Bend. Nick was a better high school quarterback than his older brother and was a scholarship player at the University of Washington; but, like his brother, when things didn't work out, he had many stops to make in his college career before calling it quits.

Montana never pushed his sons to play football. Once they made the decision to play, he never pressured them to continue, and he certainly didn't pressure them to play up to his standards. He didn't get impatient with them when they were just throwing the ball around and couldn't spin it like him. He never forced them to take their careers any further than they wanted.

It's also not easy for a Hall of Fame quarterback to instruct young quarterbacks, especially his kids. There is a surprising lack of quarterbacks who have become head coaches, and none of the four in the NFL in 2017 were very good players. Jason Garrett of the Cowboys and Doug Pederson of the Eagles were longtime NFL backup quarterbacks. Washington's Jay

Gruden was a quarterback in the Arena Football League, the World League of American Football, and the Canadian Football League; and Sean Payton of the Saints played in the Arena Football League and the Canadian Football League and was on the strike replacement-team roster of the Chicago Bears in 1987.

When Nick ended up at Tulane on the third stop of his college career and needed private instruction, Montana knew better than to do it himself. Nick went from New Orleans up to New Jersey more than five times before spring practice for his final year of college football to work with a former NFL quarterback. That quarterback happened to be Phil Simms, one of Joe Montana's most bitter rivals when Simms played for the Giants and Montana played for the 49ers. They had some monumental battles in the regular season and the play-offs.

It was quite a turn in their relationship that Joe asked Phil to work with his son. Nate came and watched. Joe was there several times. After all those games against each other at Giants Stadium and Candlestick Park, the two quarterbacks had become good friends. At Super Bowl LI in Houston in 2017, Montana and Simms made an appearance together for a sponsor. They put on a great show and played off each other well.

"When we played, we really didn't like each other," Simms told the crowd.

Montana laughed. They came to really like each other over the years, and Simms was flattered that Montana sent his son to him. Simms felt Nick had ability and wished he could have worked with him when he was in high school or earlier in his college career. His words carried impact with Nick Montana.

Montana could have been telling his son the same thing as Simms, but when advice and instruction come from a parent, it doesn't always have the same impact as it does coming from an independent voice.

"Phil was wonderful with Nicky," Montana said. "He would come home and tell stories and laugh about things that Phil would say."

But if Joe gave Nick the same advice, it would have gone in one ear and out the other. "It's weird to other people, but he's our dad; and we had the same reaction everyone does when their dad tells them something. We don't want to listen," Nick told the San José *Mercury News* when he was a freshman at Washington in 2010. "It took us a while to realize he knows what he's talking about."

In addition to his broadcasting career, Simms developed a side business of instructing high school and college quarterbacks. The careers of Montana and Simms ran side by side after both were drafted in 1979. If the Giants had not drafted Simms with the seventh overall pick, Montana might not have been drafted in San Francisco.

Bill Walsh, coach of the 49ers, wanted Simms, but the 49ers' first-round pick, the overall number 1 pick in the draft, had been traded to the Buffalo Bills in the O. J. Simpson trade before Walsh arrived in 1979. Walsh was hoping to get the little-known Simms from Morehead State in Kentucky at the top of the second round. Back in those days, before scouting became so sophisticated, it was possible for quarterback surprises in the first round. But Walsh was not the only executive who loved

Simms, and his plans were spoiled when Giants rookie general manager George Young drafted him in the first round. Walsh then waited until the 49ers closed out the third round with the eighty-second overall selection, on a pick originally owned by the Dallas Cowboys, and picked Montana over Steve Dils, who had played for Walsh at Stanford.

Walsh's version of the West Coast offense and Montana's proficiency in the short passing game, combined with his quick feet, as mesmerizing as a ballet dancer's, were a perfect match. By their third season together, they'd won their first Super Bowl; and the victory over the Cowboys, with Brady in the stands at Candlestick Park, is still the most memorable game in the history of the franchise.

When Montana's sons were ready to play football, they began a long and at times emotionally painful journey trying to live up to their father's legacy.

"Our older one wasn't quite as interested right away, whereas at the eight- or nine-year-old age my younger one was," Montana said. "Nate got off to a...later start than Nicholas did. He caught up fairly fast. It was fine with them, but it was also kind of, 'Gosh, it was hard.' There was such expectation. We go to Pop Warner with our youngest one; the head coach there, he only let his son play quarterback and nobody else took snaps the whole time."

Montana was no longer playing in the NFL, but he remained an iconic figure in the Bay Area, where he was still living. He knew what the coach was doing wasn't right. Montana doesn't have a pushy personality, but his presence can be intimidating.

Was the coach trying to prove something? Joe Montana's kid was a quarterback, but so was the coach's son. Power can be a dangerous thing.

"I said to him, 'If your son gets hurt, you're going to have a problem because no one is taking snaps,'" Montana said. "I told him Nicholas throws the ball pretty well and you're going to need to have somebody else."

After one practice, Montana confronted the coach again.

"Did Nicholas take any snaps?" he said.

"We tried to get him to take a snap before practice, but he was like two feet away and he bent down and was looking for the ball to be snapped under the guy's leg like a mini-shotgun," the coach said.

"Well, that's what he does every day," Montana said.

"Well, he doesn't know how to take a snap," the coach said.

"He's eight," Montana said.

Montana told the coach to let the kids go at their own pace. He could surely have taught Nick how to take a snap. "That's your job. You're the coach," he said. "You've got to teach them how to take a snap."

Montana was caught in a difficult situation. If he walked on the field and said, "Hey, I'm Joe Montana, I'll take over now," he would alienate the coach, the other parents, and embarrass his kids. If he stayed in the background, it would be hard to accept his kids not being treated fairly, whether it was because the coach was determined not to be influenced by having Montana's kid on the team, or the coach was protecting the interests of his own son, or just resenting Montana's presence. Instead of being embraced as Joe Montana, 49ers hero, it worked against him and his kids.

"Those are the kinds of things that happened all along the way. It's just hard," Montana said. "There's a lot more expectations."

That was something he did not have to face growing up. His father, Joe Sr., would come to practices and encourage him, but once he started playing games, Joe Sr. didn't know enough about football to provide any assistance. However, there once came a point when Joe was eleven years old that he wanted to quit playing in the middle of the season. His father said that was unacceptable.

"He said just because it gets hard, you don't want to quit, you don't want to give up," Montana said. "If I wanted to quit, he said I could at the end of the season. I ended up going back."

Why did he want to quit?

"I hated running sprints," he said.

Second-generation quarterbacks are rare in the NFL. Of course, the Mannings are considered the First Family of Football. Archie, the patriarch, played fourteen years with the Saints, Oilers, and Vikings, and never made the play-offs. Peyton was in the NFL for eighteen seasons and won and lost a Super Bowl with the Colts and won and lost a Super Bowl with the Broncos. In his first thirteen seasons, Eli beat the Patriots twice in the Super Bowl in his only two Super Bowl appearances.

Archie was just as talented, if not more talented, than either of his sons, and for sure he was a better athlete. He had the misfortune, though, of playing on consistently lousy teams. No matter how the Manning quarterbacks are ranked one through three, they were each great players.

Andrew Luck of the Indianapolis Colts has been superior to his father, Oliver, who at one time was Archie Manning's backup in Houston. Bob Griese won two Super Bowls with the Dolphins, while his son Brian won a national championship for Michigan playing ahead of Brady in 1997. Brian Griese had minimal success taking over in Denver after John Elway retired. Griese played for four teams, and the Bucs twice.

Chris Simms never won a play-off game in his eight years in the NFL with the Bucs, Broncos, and Titans; and Matt Simms has had a hard time getting off the practice squads of the Jets, Bills, and Falcons. Their father, Phil, played one of the great Super Bowls of all time.

There's also David Whitehurst and his son, Charlie, each of whom were career backups.

Nate and Nick Montana wanted to play. Joe didn't push them.

"No, not at all," Joe said. "We let them say, 'We want to play.' After that, you try to help as much as you can. As they get older, you say, 'This is what you need to do; if you are not doing this, I can't help you. I won't come here and sit here and make you do it. If you don't want to do it, you will never do it no matter how much I try to help you.' Kids in this day and age, with the Internet and the computer, you have to battle. They both went on their own path and they both found their way. There was never a happier day for Jennifer [than] when they both said, 'This is it.'"

Joe and model/actress Jennifer Wallace were married in 1985 after they met doing a Schick razor commercial. One year later, Montana suffered the first serious injury of his career when he required back surgery to repair a herniated disk and missed two months of the season. An elbow injury in 1991 gave Steve Young the opening to take his job, and Montana was traded to the Chiefs after the 1992 season. He suffered a concussion playing for Kansas City in the 1993 AFC Championship Game and retired the following season after a play-off loss to Dan Marino and the Dolphins.

Montana has had major back surgery in his retirement years, the result of the punishment he took playing football his entire life. "Jennifer has seen what I went through," he said. "Other players I played with or [have] seen at the Hall of Fame have struggled with a lot of the same things."

When Nate and Nick decided not to play football anymore, it was a burden lifted from the entire Montana family.

|||||||||||||||||||||||||||||||||||||||||||||||||

Nate Montana was first in line trying to live up to being the son of Joe Montana, football icon.

By the time he was ready for high school, he was all-in on football. He started off at Cardinal Newman in Santa Rosa but was buried on the quarterback depth chart. He transferred his senior year to De La Salle High School in Concord, California, where it was going to be even tougher for him to get playing time. De La Salle has a great football tradition and annually has one of the best football teams in the country, but it turned out to be a bad experience. It is a football powerhouse, and it's highly competitive just to get on the field. It has produced a long list of professional athletes, including several students who went on to the NFL. Wide receiver Amani Toomer, running back Maurice Jones-Drew, and safety T. J. Ward are among the De La Salle grads.

"Nate played very rarely," Joe Montana said.

As a result, Nate didn't have much of an opportunity to impress college recruiters. It's a hard thing to do from the bench. He was 12 of 19 for 166 yards and a single touchdown in his one year at De La Salle. "There was no playing time. Not just for him, but a lot of the kids," Montana said.

Did he deserve to play? "He would outthrow everybody," Joe said. "They were going for the rankings. They say it's about the kids, but it was about trying to be the number 1 team in the nation. They were playing one team in central California. That school had only twenty-six players on their roster. De La Salle didn't substitute until they were up by almost 50, which is ridiculous. That is what was so disheartening."

When Nate was a senior, Nick was a sophomore. They were both backup quarterbacks at De La Salle.

"Can we get out of here?" Jennifer said to Joe. "I'm dying a slow death."

If Nick was going to have any chance to be recruited to a big-time college football program, the Montanas were convinced he had to leave De La Salle. Nate's experience was torture for all of them. Besides running the option offense, which is unfriendly to quarterbacks who like to throw the ball, their experience with the program had been anything but positive. The Montanas couldn't technically have Nick change high schools to switch for the football program, but Joe and Jennifer and Nick got around that by moving from the Bay Area to Southern California, and Nick enrolled at Oaks Christian School in Westlake Village, California, about fifty miles northwest of Los Angeles.

The next town over is Thousand Oaks, where the Dallas Cowboys held training camp for many years at Cal-Lutheran University. The Los Angeles Rams, after moving back from St. Louis in 2016, set up their offices and training facility in Thousand Oaks on the campus of Cal-Lutheran.

Two of Nick's teammates at Oaks Christian were Trevor Gretzky, the son of hockey Hall of Famer Wayne Gretzky; and Trey Smith, the son of actor Will Smith. Gretzky was the backup quarterback to Nick. Smith was a wide receiver. The star power in the bleachers exceeded the football talent on the field. They nicknamed the school "Hollywood High."

It wasn't long after Nick's transition to his new school as the starting quarterback that Joe had an emptiness inside he knew could not be fixed. He felt guilty for not moving Nate out of De La Salle and enrolling him at Oaks Christian.

"We looked at Thousand Oaks earlier for Nathaniel also and we probably should have put him there because it was a better fit," he said. "De La Salle just wasn't a good fit for either one of them. They don't run the option; they are not option quarterbacks. Nicholas benefited from the mistake we made unfortunately with Nathaniel."

Nate's lack of playing time in high school led to his deciding to attend Notre Dame without a scholarship. Joe had some talks with Weis, the Notre Dame head coach, who was a former assistant coach with the New York Giants, New York Jets, and New England Patriots. Weis had a reputation as a quarterback guru. He was the offensive coordinator when the Patriots drafted Brady in 2000 and was given a lot of credit for his development.

If Nate was looking to escape from his father's shadow, he picked the wrong school. He could have walked on anywhere and the chances of starting would have been just as prohibitive. But choosing his father's school, where Joe had lifetime superhero status after leading the Fighting Irish to the 1977 national championship, and entering competition against highly recruited quarterbacks, didn't make sense from a football perspective. He was given preferred walk-on status. Then Weis gave him number 16, and even though Notre Dame's home jerseys were blue and the 49ers' were a deep red, there was quite a similarity. On the back was the big numeral 16 below the name Montana.

Nate didn't decide on Notre Dame because his father had played there thirty years earlier. His older sisters Alexandra and Elizabeth had each recently graduated from there. "I would frequently visit them and go to games. I just fell in love with the university itself," he said. "The atmosphere, the way the campus was, the game atmosphere, it sucked me in at a young age. That was the main decision-making point. There were definitely some other schools [where] I could have taken the same path as Notre Dame. It was tough to have an unbiased view of other schools when I had great childhood memories of the university."

He did not throw one pass as a freshman in 2008, not unusual for a walk-on. He transferred to Pasadena City College after his freshman year and was able to play a bit. He threw 88 passes. Nick decided to return to Notre Dame after the season and was back on campus in January 2010. Weis had been fired as head coach and was replaced by Brian Kelly. "They gave him a scholarship after Kelly's first spring," Montana said. "He had a pretty good spring game, actually better than the other quarterbacks. He was happy as a clam and that's all you can ask for. Here's a kid who didn't play in high school and all of a sudden he played well in the spring game and they gave him a scholarship."

In the Blue-Gold spring game, Montana had his best moments at Notre Dame. He was 18 of 30 for 223 yards and three touchdowns, leading the Gold team to a 27–19 victory. When the season opened, however, junior Dayne Crist was the starting quarterback. He led Notre Dame to a season-opening victory over Purdue.

The next week, the usual 80,795 fans filled Notre Dame Stadium. Joe and Jennifer Montana were sitting in a bar in Seattle watching the game. They were in town visiting Nick, a freshman who was being redshirted at Washington with the expectation that he would be the starter the next year. Joe jumped out of his chair and had to be calmed down by Jennifer when Number 16 came running onto the field in the first quarter against Michigan after Crist was injured.

Nate Montana had his big chance. Crist was sidelined for most of the first half with blurry vision. Freshman Tommy Rees was first off the bench, but he was pulled after throwing 2 passes with one of them intercepted. Finally, Montana was getting his opportunity on a big stage against a big-time opponent.

In the final moments of the first half, he connected with Theo Riddick on a 37-yard pass that put the Irish at the Michigan 3-yard line. They trailed 21–7. Just three seconds were left in the half. Instead of putting points on the board and kicking a 20-yard field goal, Kelly elected to run a play and go for the touchdown. Montana's pass sailed out of the end zone. Crist returned to the game in the second half and Notre Dame rallied but lost 28–24.

"When you leave high school and all of a sudden find yourself in your first game, Notre Dame–Michigan tied up 7–7 in the first quarter, and you haven't played since high school, you're in a really tough situation," Joe Montana said. "He handled it in the beginning just like anyone else would. He was a little nervous, then settled down and made a couple of things happen right before halftime. Then the coach made a mistake and he blamed it on him. He should have kicked the field goal. You have an unseasoned quarterback with three seconds to go. You don't make him throw one of the hardest passes there is."

Montana was 8 of 17 for 104 yards with one interception. When Crist suffered a season-ending knee injury in November that year, he was replaced by Rees. Montana played in two more games and threw only one more pass in his Notre Dame career, a 12-yard completion. Kelly wanted him to move to safety, but he was not interested. He was not the next Joe Cool and had to deal with unfulfilled expectations at his father's school.

"I just kind of let it roll off," Nate said. "You can't add any weight to it or you will then be in a mental battle with yourself with all the added pressure of being there and being the quarterback at that university. You have to try to mitigate as many negative influences as you can. I had experiences with that growing up."

Rather than move to safety, he transferred to the University of Montana—seems appropriate—for one year and left after throwing just 42 passes, then finished up with one year at West Virginia Wesleyan, a Division II school. But at least he had a team to call his own. He threw for 2,480 yards and nineteen touchdowns.

Montana was the typical dad watching his sons play. Nervous, anxious, hoping they would succeed.

"It was a lot of fun, to a certain degree," he told the *Mercury News*. "The other part can be heart-wrenching at times. I know exactly what their emotions are, whether they're up or down, and that makes it tough. You hope they never make a mistake, but you also know that can never be the case. There isn't anyone who can experience that, who can go through it with them, unless you've played the position."

Nate had some drinking issues in college. He was one of eleven Notre Dame athletes arrested for underage drinking in 2010 and then was arrested in Montana in 2011 for suspicion of driving under the influence. The charges were later dropped.

He was not drafted after finishing up at West Virginia

Wesleyan, but he was invited to a regional combine in Dallas. He had been working with George Whitfield, a well-known quarterback coach in San Diego. But in the spring game of his senior year, Nate had ankle surgery and an Achilles injury, and when he went to the combine Joe was told by Gil Brandt, the former Cowboys vice president, that Nate was just not healthy.

The 49ers were the only team that invited Nate in for a tryout. He dressed in the same locker room in their Santa Clara facility as his father once did. He took part in a pro day, attended a rookie minicamp on a tryout basis, and was invited back for a one-day rookie minicamp. That was the end of his football career.

"I have no regrets whatsoever," he said. "I gave it a good effort. I gave myself a good timeline of how long I would try and pursue it. If it didn't work out, I was not pigeonholed. I happily moved on. I miss some of the aspects of football. The locker room, the team camaraderie, seeing your good friends on a daily basis. But I have a lot of other competitive outlets."

||||||||||||||||||||||||||||||||||||||||||||

Nick Montana was a highly recruited quarterback out of Oaks Christian. The Montana family relocated from their five-hundred-acre estate in Calistoga in the Bay Area to Thousand Oaks, enabling Nick to transfer from De La Salle to Oaks Christian. Joe felt that he hadn't put Nate in the best position to succeed and wanted to give his younger son a better opportunity.

It was a prudent decision. Nick earned the starting job at Oaks

Christian and passed for 2,404 yards and thirty-three touchdowns as a junior. He became a hot recruit and had attractive options to pick from in deciding where he wanted to go to college. Alabama (Nick Saban); Stanford (Jim Harbaugh); Ohio State (Jim Tressel); and South Carolina (Steve Spurrier) offered him scholarships. So did Notre Dame (Kelly); LSU (Les Miles); Georgia (Mark Richt); Nebraska (Bo Pelini); and Florida State (which was transitioning from Bobby Bowden to Jimbo Fisher). That was an impressive list. Joe traveled with him on some of his visits.

Nick Montana picked the University of Washington, coached by Steve Sarkisian, and phoned him in June prior to his senior year to inform him of his decision. Sarkisian was a highly regarded offensive coach who had been on the national championship staff of Pete Carroll at the University of Southern California.

The Montana family was certainly hoping Nick's college career would be a much smoother ride and more satisfying than Nate's. He was a better player and better prepared to play in college. After making his college decision, Nick had an outstanding senior season at Oaks Christian, throwing for 2,636 yards and thirty-four touchdowns. In two years, he was 27-1 as the starting quarterback. Scout.com ranked him as the number 300 overall high school prospect in the country and the number 19 quarterback. He was such a hyped prospect that when Oaks Christian went up to Seattle to play Skyline High School, which had its own top quarterback prospect in Jake Heap, the game was televised on ESPN.

He enrolled at Washington in time for spring ball before

his freshman year in 2010. The Huskies were all set at quarterback for one more year with senior Jake Locker, and Montana wanted to set himself up to be first in line to succeed him in 2011. Locker would be a first-round pick by the Tennessee Titans. Montana was on the traveling team as a backup quarterback as a freshman, but he did not play in any games. He served as a game captain for two games, but because he did not see any game action, Sarkisian redshirted him, meaning he still had four years of eligibility remaining. Redshirting is a familiar practice. Brady was redshirted his freshman year at Michigan. If a player is injured and misses the entire season, he can be redshirted. That's what happened with Joe Montana at Notre Dame when he separated his shoulder before his junior year, giving him one more year of eligibility.

Nick Montana had lost out to Keith Price, one year ahead of him as a redshirt sophomore, to be Locker's backup. Once Locker was gone, the Huskies had an opening for the starting quarterback job. Once again, Price beat out Montana. Nick Montana played in six of Washington's thirteen games in 2011, with one start when Price was sidelined with a knee injury. He completed 11 of 21 passes for 79 yards and two touchdowns in a 38–21 loss to Oregon State. But Price had 33 touchdown passes in his first year as the starter and was secure as the number 1 going forward. Montana realized that Price had two years of eligibility remaining, and if Price didn't declare early for the NFL Draft, then he had no path to play until his senior year. Even then, he would face competition from younger players on the roster.

Price was a very good college quarterback who would go on to get a free agent tryout with the Seattle Seahawks and then have a long career in the Canadian Football League. Montana decided he had to get out of Washington. Just like his older brother, he was in a situation where he saw no opportunity to play. It is always difficult to project what will be the best fit, but Washington seemed like a good idea at the time. Who knows what would have happened if Montana had gone to play for Harbaugh at Stanford? Harbaugh left in 2011 to coach the 49ers. Tressel would be replaced by Urban Meyer at Ohio State. It's also impossible to predict how the competition will develop.

After two years on campus, it was time for another of Joe's sons to transfer.

"I've got three years left and I want to spend those on the field," Nick said to the *Seattle Times*. "I don't want to wait another year. You only get one shot at playing college football. I just made the best decision for me and I'm going with it."

Joe and Jennifer backed Nick. "They just wanted the best for me," he said. "I just wanted to get on the field anywhere. They were super supportive of that."

His plan was to go to a junior college for one year to get playing time and then attend another four-year school. He enrolled at Mount San Antonio College in Walnut, California, a suburb of Los Angeles. It has nearly fifty-eight thousand students and is one of the largest community colleges in California. Several NFL players have stopped off there on the way to major college football, including linebacker Antonio Pierce, who later enrolled at the University of Arizona and played for the

Washington Redskins and New York Giants, where he was the defensive captain of their 2007 Super Bowl championship team. Cornerback Chris McAlister took the same route to the University of Arizona and played on the Baltimore Ravens 2000 Super Bowl championship team.

After one year at Mount San Antonio, Montana enrolled at Tulane. That made it a total of seven colleges between him and his brother. Nick was named the starter soon after he arrived in New Orleans.

He threw for 1,717 yards with fourteen touchdowns and ten interceptions before separating his shoulder. He came back and led Tulane to its first bowl game in twelve years. His parents accumulated a lot of frequent-flier miles attending all of his home games. By the next spring, his final year of eligibility, he was back on the bench after losing his job to redshirt freshman Tanner Lee. Montana started two games when Lee was out with a shoulder injury. Tulane coach Curtis Johnson promised Nick two series on Senior Night, and with his parents and brother at the game, Nick threw for 42 yards and led Tulane on its only scoring drive in a 10–3 loss to Temple. One year after Montana was gone from Tulane, so was Lee. He transferred to Nebraska after Johnson was fired and the new coach, Willie Fritz from Georgia Southern, installed the option offense. Lee was from New Orleans, which Joe Montana says had factored into Johnson's decision to bench his son. When his career ended at Tulane, Nick was done with football.

"I think the thing you wish for is only that they get a fair chance and a fair opportunity and people don't have expectations or have other agendas, which kind of happened in Tulane," he said. "Just let them win or lose it as their ability dictates. Don't try to play someone because you want to play local kids. They put in a kid who led the nation in interceptions, and interceptions run back for touchdowns. They never took the kid out once. It was a local kid. That was the head coach's mission at the time, to play local kids. I tried to explain to him that you will get the good local kids when you start winning. You've got to find a way to win, but you can't do that when a guy is throwing that many interceptions."

This is not what Nick Montana signed up for when he decided to attend Tulane. But he didn't get what he expected at Washington, either. His football career was over. He didn't get drafted and was not asked to attend any NFL tryouts. It was time to move on from football. He was actually relieved that football was over.

"Honestly, after going through all that, it became more stress. I lost the fun out of the game," he said. "Until my last year at Tulane, when they did make the switch; that took all the pressure off and I actually enjoyed it more. When I started the games I did as a senior, I had so much fun. I didn't really care anymore, to be completely honest. I had more fun with my teammates and coaches and more fun on the field."

He thought about that for a second. Isn't that the way sports should be? Isn't that what football is all about? Bonding with teammates and coaches and fighting together in a team sport?

"If I have any regret," Nick Montana said, "it's not playing like that my whole life."

Joe Montana

IIIIIIIIIIIIIIIIIIIIIIIIIIIIIIIIIIIIIIIIIIII

Joe Montana won a national championship at Notre Dame and four Super Bowls with the 49ers. He raised two sons who wanted to be just like him. If their last names were Wallace, as they put on their uniforms as young kids to try to become somewhat anonymous, their nomadic lives as college quarterbacks would have gone pretty much unnoticed.

Nate was just a walk-on at Notre Dame, and earning a scholarship was a great accomplishment. Nick had major colleges from all over the country recruiting him; he picked Washington and then got beat out by a better player. The pressure was intense carrying the Montana name, but that was not the reason they didn't live up to expectations.

They both are bigger physically than their father and were better built to play quarterback. They just lacked his talent. The standard their father set in his Hall of Fame career has been surpassed by only one quarterback, and that's Tom Brady. To think Nate or Nick could come close to what their father accomplished—well, the odds were insurmountable.

That's what makes the Manning family so unique. Archie had a great career but played for bad teams. Peyton and Eli have each won two Super Bowls; and, adding in the two that Peyton lost, the Manning boys have played in six. Archie always says he didn't raise his sons to be quarterbacks. Neither did Joe Montana.

"It's good to see both of them made it," Joe said. "They had done what they wanted to do and how they wanted to do it.

They both worked hard at getting to where they were. It ended differently for both. Like Jennifer says, it built great character for both of them, having to fight through issues and seeing how the world works from a different point of view." Not once did Joe ever express disappointment that his sons failed to achieve as he did on the football field. He was disappointed for them, but he never felt that they let him down.

"Never ever for a second would he say he was disappointed or anything along those lines," Nate said. "He was there to support us. That never changed."

Nick was not even three when his father's career ended. Nate was a couple of months past his fifth birthday. He has a vague recollection of going to one game in Kansas City in the final two years of Joe's career. "Just a brief mental picture," he said.

In turn, Joe remembers Nate running on the field at Notre Dame Stadium for the first time wearing number 16. "Just how proud he was," Joe said.

Nate now works for an investment fund that his father started. Nick has a job in the financial industry. They each live in San Francisco. They have come to appreciate how great a quarterback their father was and how much he accomplished. Joe used to show them instructional videos he did with Bill Walsh. Nick remembers a stack of DVDs of old games in a cabinet and popping them into an old video recorder to watch some of Joe's magic.

"I just remember it taking my breath away. He was unbelievable," Nick said.

"To be able to achieve what he did at that level, it makes a clear case that he's one of [the greatest], if not the greatest, to play that position," Nate said. "To be perfect in the Super Bowl—no interceptions, no losses, three and deservedly four MVPs—it's not hard to acknowledge how good he was."

He was a great player. He's been a great dad, too.

ACKNOWLEDGMENTS

Joe Montana's first Super Bowl was number XVI. So was mine.

When I was in Houston to witness Tom Brady's dramatic comeback in Super Bowl XLI in 2017, it was the thirty-sixth consecutive Super Bowl that I've covered, and I have seen some truly amazing games. The Bears' complete annihilation of the Patriots. Phil Simms's near perfection against the Broncos. Joe Montana noticing John Candy in the stands in Miami and then driving the 49ers the length of the field to beat the Bengals. Scott Norwood's wide right.

John Elway's first Super Bowl victory after three lopsided losses. Adam Vinatieri's game-winner in Brady's first championship. David Tyree's "Helmet Catch." Santonio Holmes's tip-toe on the sidelines. Pete Carroll not giving Marshawn Lynch the ball against the Patriots. Dwight Clark's "Catch" in the 1981 National Football Conference Championship Game was the first unforgettable football game I ever covered.

I was there for Game 4 of the 1969 World Series when my Mets beat the Baltimore Orioles to take a commanding 3–1 series lead. I've seen the Mets play in person in Game 1 of the 1986 World Series and Game 3 of the 2015 World Series.

I was there when Michael Jordan hit the game-winner in the 1982 NCAA Championship Game against Georgetown at the Superdome in New Orleans. I was also in Providence in 1975 when Syracuse, my alma mater, beat North Carolina and Kansas State to advance to the Final Four when I was sports editor of the *Daily Orange*.

Okay, so I've been lucky enough to see some big-time sports moments in my time.

It's hard for me to decide which from that collection is second on my greatest games list. None of them come close to my number 1.

It was the spring of 2013. Horace Greeley High School of Chappaqua, New York, versus Ossining High School, in the first round of the baseball play-offs. On the mound for Greeley was seventeen-year-old right-handed pitcher Andrew Myers. Good fastball. Excellent changeup. Knee-buckling curve.

Greeley had not won a play-off game since 2006. To say I was nervous, well, I was wearing out the grass as I paced before the game. Unless Greeley was going to go on an unlikely play-off run, this was going to be the last time I saw my son pitch in high school. I coached his teams in Little League and can count on one hand the number of games I missed from the time he was five right through high school. One of my great thrills was being a fan at a tournament he participated in with his summer travel team in 2008 down the street from the baseball Hall of Fame in Cooperstown. They played nine games in four days, and he started three games and pitched in relief in three games. Amazingly, he didn't require Tommy John surgery.

I have two older daughters who played softball. Michelle also played freshman field hockey. Emily can really smack a golf ball. I coached many of their softball teams. In fact, one year I coached each of their softball teams and my son's baseball team. That was nuts.

Baseball was my favorite sport as a kid, and I still love it. I cherished the times when Andrew would ask me to have a catch in the backyard. I know how Jack Harbaugh felt. On hot summer weekends, we would drive over to the high school and I would pitch to him or hit him grounders and fly balls and squat down and he would throw a bullpen session—until he started throwing too hard and it was no longer in my best interests to catch him. Even when he gave me the sign that the curveball was coming, I had no chance.

I can only imagine now what it was like for Archie Manning to see his sons Peyton and Eli win the Super Bowl in consecutive seasons. Or for Tom Brady Sr. to see his son win five Super Bowls. Wow.

Back to Ossining High School. This was my Super Bowl. My Game 7 of the World Series. This was a *My First Coach* moment. Every pitch mattered, every at bat was huge.

Through three innings, Andrew was throwing a no-hitter. But Greeley didn't have many big bats, so it was scoreless. In the top of the fourth, we scored two runs. The way he was pitching, that looked good enough to stand up. In the bottom of the fourth, Ossining got its first hit and then had runners on second and third with two out. Andrew tried to blow a fastball by the hitter, who swung late and hit a soft line drive just over the glove of the leaping second baseman. Both runners were on the move with two outs and scored. Score tied 2–2.

Greeley got a clutch two-out hit in the top of the seventh to take a 3–2 lead. It was on to the bottom of the seventh and last inning. Andrew was still throwing hard. He had given up three hits and struck out seven. Now there was one out to go. Clean single to the outfield. The center fielder kicked it around and the runner wound up on second. It was a good thing there were no blood pressure machines in the parent section. Mine was probably at 200/125.

The coach came out to the mound. There was action in the bullpen. Coach asked Andrew how he was doing.

"This is my game," he said. He goes 0-2 on the next hitter. Then a called third strike for his eighth K.

All the practices and all the games over the years were always worth it no matter what. But this was his greatest athletic achievement and instantly became the greatest game I've ever witnessed. Forget the Super Bowls when it's your own kid. The postgame hug will last a lifetime.

That was the inspiration for *My First Coach*, which was actually suggested by Andrew when he thought about our relationship. After he read my *Brady vs Manning* book and about the relationship between Archie and Peyton and Tom Sr. and Tom, the idea was planted to explore the dynamic between quarterbacks and their fathers.

It started me on a journey that was so enjoyable. I loved hearing the stories of how kids like my son who developed the skills and size to be quarterbacks were nurtured and supported by their fathers. The life lessons that would be learned from the experiences of the players fortunate enough to take it to the highest level hopefully will provide inspiration and motivation for boys and girls and their mothers and fathers.

I have written a lot over the years about Archie's relationship with Peyton, the younger brother to Cooper and older brother to Eli. This time we talked about how parents deal with a third child and whether experiencing the same events for a third time as a parent lessens the enthusiasm. Archie loves to tell stories and I love to listen to them.

I went to see Joe Flacco at the Baltimore Ravens facility in Owings Mills, Maryland. The only time I had spoken to Joe was in a group setting at the Super Bowl a few years earlier. He's just a kid from south Jersey who happened to have an incredible arm. We laughed about the Brady poster that is still hanging on the wall of the bedroom he shared with his younger brother Mike. His father, Steve, was passionate talking about Joe, and you can feel his frustration when he talks about how his son was treated at Pitt.

Ask Jim Harbaugh who his starting quarterback is going to be and he tells you to wait and see who is in the huddle. Ask him about his dad, Jack, and he can talk all day about how he tries to make him proud every day. Jim played at Michigan after his father was an assistant coach for Bo Schembechler, and now that Jim is back in Ann Arbor in Bo's old job, his parents have moved in right around the corner. How cool is that?

The football careers of Montana's sons ended after college. I want to thank Joe for being so open with me about the pressure his boys were under to live up to the Montana name. He even had Nate and Nick call me one day, and the three of us had a roundtable discussion about their lives as the sons of one of the greatest quarterbacks of all time.

I could sit and talk to Phil Simms for hours, and as we visited in his home office in Franklin Lakes, New Jersey, I remembered the first time I met Simms. The Giants had drafted him in the first round in 1979. This was before the days of Mel Kiper, so nobody outside New York had ever heard of Simms. When the Giants brought him in for his first press conference, a photographer asked Simms to sign his name on a chalkboard in the basement press room that we called the Dungeon at Giants stadium. Simms signed with his left hand.

"Oh no, did the Giants know he is a lefty?" somebody said. Simms was indeed a righty; he just writes with his left hand.

John Elway told me poignant stories about his father, Jack. Jameis "Jaboo" Winston and his dad, Antonor "Ant" Winston, have a special relationship. Nothing was as intriguing as the entire Carr family moving to Houston when David was drafted and how little brother Derek adjusted to life in Texas and then moved back to California for his senior year of high school. The great thing about Ryan Fitzpatrick is that he's so smart— Harvard, class of 2005—football is often the last thing I want to talk to him about.

Acknowledgments

I want to thank all the quarterbacks and their dads for being so generous with their time. And for being so forthcoming as well.

Generosity is one thing; patience is another. Nobody has more patience than my editor, Sean Desmond, the best in the business. Anybody who can go from editing George W. Bush's *Decision Points* to editing my football books is indeed versatile and talented. He may have allowed me to push the deadline back a couple of times, but he never seemed too upset. Or at least he didn't tell me.

Major thanks to Kevin Byrne of the Ravens, Dave Ablauf at Michigan, Will Kiss of the Raiders, Nelson Luis of the Bucs, Bruce Speight of the Jets, Corry Rush of the Giants, and Patrick Smyth of the Broncos for helping to set up interviews; and thanks to the quarterbacks for getting me in touch with their fathers.

Now it can be told: Harbaugh is one of the reasons I didn't get enough writing done during the 2016 season. It was also my son's senior year at Michigan and I was totally caught up watching the Wolverines every Saturday afternoon. If they weren't so good, I wouldn't have been watching.

As I left Harbaugh's office on the second floor of Schembechler Hall one week before the 2016 season, he asked me when the book would be coming out.

"Right before the 2017 season," I said. "When you guys are the defending national champions."

He smiled. Well, if they had beaten Ohio State, it might have happened. Maybe next year, Coach.

Of course, I want to thank my wife, Allison, forever my best friend. I can still hear her words rattling around in my head whenever I decided I needed a day off. "You have a book to write," she said.

Yes, I did. She was right, as usual. And it got done, just like I told her it would.

My three kids are my greatest inspiration. Michelle is a nutritionist at a world-renowned cancer hospital. Emily is involved in health and safety and is trying to help make football safer for this and the next generation. Andrew's goal is to run a major-league baseball team, and I have no doubt he will do it.

Of course, I want to thank my parents, who sacrificed to make life better for me. I think about you every day.

Raising a quarterback doesn't come with a manual. The first obligation is instilling values to be good people, to treat people right, to never take anything for granted, and to work hard. If they are blessed to have the athletic skills to be an athlete, that is a bonus. Then it's up to the parents to give their sons—or daughters, of course, in other sports—the guidance and wisdom to take their talents to playing college and professional football.

It becomes complicated finding the balance between school and athletics when there is naturally no guarantee anybody's quarterback is going to be good enough to make it to the NFL. All a parent can do is put their child in the best position to succeed and hope they can stay injury-free, have coaches who don't have an agenda, and are able to fulfill their potential.

Acknowledgments

Phil Simms was able to overcome an alcoholic father to become a Super Bowl champion. John Elway and Jim Harbaugh grew up in football homes with college coaches as their dads, giving them a head start learning the game. But for Elway to play in five Super Bowls and for Harbaugh to play fifteen years in the NFL, it took more than their fathers being in the business. Jameis Winston needed the strong support of his father to help get him through some serious issues, but even though he has now made it to the NFL, he is still a young man who needs his father.

My First Coach has been an educational journey. There are plenty of ways to raise a quarterback. There is no playbook.

INDEX

Index

Index

Index

Index

ABOUT THE AUTHOR

Gary Myers is the NFL columnist for the New York *Daily News*. He has authored three books: *The Catch,* a look at the iconic 1981 NFC Championship Game between the Cowboys and 49ers; *Coaching Confidential,* which details the pressures of being an NFL head coach; and the *New York Times* bestseller *Brady vs Manning,* an inside look at one of the greatest rivalries in NFL history. Myers has been covering the NFL since 1978. He was a member of the cast of HBO's *Inside the NFL* and the YES Network s *This Week in Football.* Currently the host of WFAN's "Chalk Talk," he is a voter for the Pro Football Hall of Fame and a former adjunct professor at Syracuse University. His own experiences coaching and watching his three kids play sports was the inspiration for *My First Coach.*